W9-CEU-548

PRAISE FOR *ALWAYS EAT LEFT HANDED*

"If humor is contagious, Rohit's new book is positively addictive. Funny, insightful, and perfectly unexpected, *Always Eat Left Handed* is the most entertaining 'business book' I've read this year. Read this and learn why doing things wrong might be the best way to be right."

—DAN ROAM, author of *Draw To Win*

"Filled with compelling stories and unexpected insights, this book exposes how most self-books that share career advice are cliché. Bhargava's book is a rare treat with an illuminating point of view you probably haven't heard before. I adored this book."

—NANCY DUARTE, CEO of Duarte, Inc. and best-selling author

"The opposite of just about any career advice book I've ever read. Make people cry. Ignore your job. Start smoking. Each suggestion felt unbelievable ... until I read it. Now I recommend this book to all my employees, interns, suppliers and anyone else I know who can use a jolt of brutal honesty on their path to being more successful."

—BEN TUBUO, VP of Supplier Diversity – Walt Disney Company

"This no-nonsense guide will help you make better decisions about your future and avoid the most common mistakes people have when they are first starting out in their careers."

—DAN SCHAWBEL, New York Times bestselling author

"Most career advice books are boring, useless, or still stuck in the 1990s. Not this one. Rohit Bhargava has written a counterintuitive, smart, and entertaining career guide that's relevant and necessary—for today."

—DORIE CLARK, author of *Reinventing You* and *Stand Out*, and adjunct professor at Duke University's Fuqua School of Business

"After years of studying people and the decisions they make, I treat any self-help advice with a healthy skepticism. This book was different. The stories had me hooked from the start. What surprised me even more was the fact that despite the non-scientific tone of the book, every secret was firmly rooted in the principles of behavioral science. In other words ... they work. Buy this book for anyone in your life who you would like to see make better decisions."

—FRANCESCA GINO, Author of *Sidetracked* and Tandon Family Professor of Business Administration, Harvard Business School

"Ever wonder what it actually takes to build an amazing network? This book goes beyond the hype and provides a unique and actionable guide on how to surround yourself with amazing people, connect authentically with them, and build the network you've always dreamed of."

—CLARA SHIH, Founder and CEO of Hearsay Systems and Member, Starbucks Board Of Directors

"*Always Eat Left Handed* is a wonderfully accessible book of small non-obvious things that anyone can put into practice. Although it is applicable to any field and age, Rohit's advice is especially good for the world-weary young millennial, who has had it up to their eyeballs with well-meaning advice. It's a rich collection of entirely snackable content that showcases how small changes can lead to big shifts in how one experiences life and work."

—GABRIELLA MIRABELLI, CEO Anatomy & Host Up Next Podcast

"Whether you are just getting started or changing careers, the beautiful lesson of this compelling book is the tiny intentional choices you make every day matter more than you think. This powerful little book will help you break down barriers, stand out and get the success you deserve every single day."

—GLORIA BELL, Co-Founder, Women in Tech

"Where was this book when I was starting out my career? This would have reduced my learning curve by a decade. A concise, refreshing read that should be mandatory for those entering the 'real-world' that could use a hand, maybe even a left one."

—SCOTT STRATTEN, President, UnMarketing Inc, Best Selling Author of 4 books, Left-Handed at Golf, Baseball, Hockey

"Careers of the 21st century will require speed, multitasking and creativity. If I were 20 again, I would bet my success on advice from someone who has spent his life looking at future trends and non-obvious insights. That person is Rohit and that book is *Always Eat Left Handed*."

—PAMELA SLIM, author of *Escape from Cubicle Nation*

"In this engaging and easy-to-read book, Rohit lays out the secrets anyone can use to get ahead and make a big difference in their life and work - simply by being a little different from the rest!"

—MELANIE NOTKIN, founder and bestselling author of *Savvy Auntie* and *Otherhood: Modern Women Finding a New Kind of Happiness*

"If you are tired of reading self-help books that try to teach you how to succeed by playing the same game as everyone else, this book offers a different approach. Like my in-person conversations over coffee with Rohit, this book will entertain and inspire you to be more intentional about how you find joy and success in every part of your life – and fulfillment through the journey you take to get there as well."

—MALLIKA CHOPRA, Author of *Living With Intent*

"If you are trying to build a compelling personal brand for yourself, this book will help you along that journey. Surprising, quirky and occasionally outrageous ... this is the most fun collection of career advice I have ever read."

—PORTER GALE, Author of *Your Network Is Your Net Worth*

"Want to know the 5 simple steps that can change your life? Actually, they don't exist. Success isn't as easy as clickbait articles make it out to be. *Always Eat Left Handed* offers much more than that. When it comes to sharing the honest truth behind what it really takes to do great stuff at work, Rohit nails it. Are you tired of overpromising miracle cures and overhyped advice? This book is for you."

MITCH JOEL, President of Mirum, author of *Six Pixels of Separation* and *CTRL ALT Delete*

Also by Rohit Bhargava

Personality Not Included:
*Why Companies Lose Their Authenticity And
How Great Brands Get it Back*

Likeonomics:
*The Unexpected Truth Behind Earning Trust,
Influencing Behavior, and Inspiring Action*

Non-Obvious:
*How To Think Different,
Curate Ideas and Predict The Future*

Always

EAt

LEFt

HANDed

15 SURPRISING SECRETS FOR KILLING IT

AT WORK AND IN REAL LIFE

ROHIT BHARGAVA

Best Selling Author of Non-Obvious

Originally published as a hardcover edition in 2017.

Published in the United States by Ideapress Publishing.

IDEAPRESS PUBLISHING | WWW.IDEAPRESSPUBLISHING.COM

All trademarks are the property of their respective companies.

COVER DESIGN BY CHRISTIE YOUNG

Cataloging-in-Publication Data is on file with the Library of Congress.

ISBN: 978-1-940858-44-9

PROUDLY PRINTED IN THE UNITED STATES OF AMERICA

BY SELBY MARKETING ASSOCIATES

SPECIAL SALES

Ideapress Books are available at a special discount for bulk purchases for sales promotions and premiums, or for use in training programs or for schools and higher education. Special editions, including personalized covers, a custom foreword, corporate imprints and bonus content are also available.

For Rohan and Jaiden,
who I hope will learn the lessons
in this book long before they need
to use them

TABLE OF CONTENTS

Is This Book for You?

Let's talk about you. Right now you are building your career, or maybe you are still finishing school... and you're surrounded by people giving you well-intentioned advice. Parents, professors, teachers, mentors and even random connections on social media all have an idea of how to help you get what you want, do what you love or supercharge your career.

You are already a master of figuring stuff out and you know that watching a YouTube video is a lot faster than reading a book. You don't describe yourself with words that fit in a neat little drop down box or any box at all. And you are highly skeptical of any book (or anyone) who offers "secrets" for being successful.

So, what can a book tell you that you can't already get from a video or buried in some of the unsolicited advice flying your way? Why should you read *this* book and how do you know it won't be a waste of your time?

The answer is one word: *non-obviousness*.

This book is written to share the opposite of what your parents, teachers and professors and bosses have been probably been telling you for years.

In the pages that follow you'll learn why it's good to interrupt often, the upside of making people cry, why it pays to be a crossdresser, how procrastinating more is the key to success, why you should start smoking and more unexpected advice like that.

My guess is that the ideas in this book (much like the word I use to describe them), will confuse some people and make many others angry. I am betting that you will not be among them.

In fact, if you've made it this far—you're probably exactly who this book is written for. Or maybe you're still curious about why to eat left handed.

Either way, keep reading to find out …

Why Eat Left Handed?

This is not a book about being left handed.

It is curious, though, just how many successful people happen to share this one trait. Left-handedness may offer a distinct advantage in everything from creative thinking to a variety of sports from boxing to bowling.

More than 25% of professional baseball players either bat or pitch left handed. Three of the last five U.S. Presidents (including George H.W. Bush, Bill Clinton, and Barack Obama) were all left handed. Lady Gaga, Steve Jobs, Bill Gates, Mark Zuckerberg, Oprah Winfrey and Jennifer Lawrence are all lefties too.

Despite only making up about 10% of the world's population, experts suggest that left-handers benefit from their uniqueness both in terms of being forced to stand out at an early age, as well as thinking differently.

In sports, the advantage is so well known that when dominant tennis legend Rafael Nadal (who is right handed) was younger, his father trained him to play left handed to get an advantage on other players.

If you happen to be left-handed, by now you're probably feeling pretty good about yourself. If you're not, don't worry … the truth is, I'm not either.

Wait a minute, what kind of author writes a book like this and starts it with all the reasons why being left handed is great when he is not even left-handed himself?

Though I am not left handed, I do actually *eat* left handed … and the story of why I do that will probably explain a lot.

HOW I DISCOVERED THE MAGIC OF EATING LEFT HANDED

It all started several years ago as I was rushing to a networking event. In my busy haste that day, I realized I had skipped lunch. As I was walking to the event, I had already created a mental plan. I would head straight to the food table, load up a plate with finger foods and find a quiet spot to eat before starting to network.

Unfortunately, my plan immediately hit a wrinkle because there weren't really any quiet spots—so I joined what appeared to be a not-so-crowded standing table. I quickly realized that shaking hands to greet anyone would be a messy affair while eating so I switched to eat with my left hand.

That simple shift made shaking hands and meeting people much easier at that table, and for the rest of the evening as well. Heading home that night, I realized the conversations from that event had somehow been better than any other event I had been to in the past several months—but I wasn't sure why. It couldn't have been the fact that I was eating left handed, could it?

Unsure but curious, I decided to try eating left handed again the following week.

When you go to a lot of networking events (as I was doing those days as part of my job), or even a lot of parties at bars or clubs to meet new people, it can be intimidating to start a conversation. Though I would describe myself as an extrovert, I was never one of those people comfortable walking up to total strangers and randomly starting a conversation. Most people aren't—even if they pretend they are.

It was at that second networking event that I realized why my connections with people had been so much better.

Eating left handed helped me change my mindset. Instead of forcing myself to start conversations with a goal of collecting as many business cards as I could, I was able to step back and just be easier to talk to. I asked more questions and listened more intently. I was in less of an impatient rush. I invited new people into conversations and focused on others instead of myself.

In a room filled with people thinking about their agendas or selling their products or finding their next employer—I accidentally became the most approachable person in the room by focusing on others instead of myself.

Since that moment, always eating left handed has become my reminder to always be generous with my time and to focus on other people. It has helped me stand out for kindness and opened up more opportunities than I could have ever imagined. And it led me to write this book.

HOW TO READ THIS BOOK

In the short chapters to come, you will read about fifteen more "secrets" like this one. Each of them is something you can do right now. You don't need special abilities to eat left handed. You don't even need *to be* left handed.

The aim of this book is to offer you a collection of approachable ideas you can use right away. It is a compilation of some of the hidden, counterintuitive, and sometimes baffling lessons that I have uncovered often by accident through a career that has included fifteen years working with some of the biggest companies in the world on branding and marketing, then walking away to start three successful businesses, write four best-selling books, travel to over thirty countries as a professional speaker, and work with some of the most inspiring and successful people in the world.

All the secrets are organized into four goals—to help you think, work, communicate and connect better—and they are shared here as a collection of stories.

If there is one theme that links them, it is that there is power in the tiny intentional choices you make every day—from what you wear to which hand you choose to eat with.

I believe making those choices deliberately can indeed help you kill it both at work (and even more importantly) in real life too.

CHAPTER 1

THE POMEGRANATE PRINCIPLE

*"Whatever happens, I can't let them
see the inside of my book."*

THIS WASN'T WHAT I EXPECTED TO BE THINKING AS I WAS GETTING
ready for my first interview to launch my new book.

It was just weeks before *Personality Not Included* would
go on bookstore shelves and already my months of planning
were being pushed off track.

The day before, my publisher McGraw-Hill had sent me
a sample of the dust jacket in advance of my planned book
tour with a short apology that the *actual* book wasn't quite
ready yet. I had a cover, no book, and my first big interview
was in less than twelve hours.

I was starting to panic. Should I cancel? Try to reschedule?
Do the interview without the book?

Finally, I had an idea. I started combing through my bookshelf to see if I had another book that was about the same thickness and dimensions as my soon-to-be-completed book. I found one and wrapped the jacket over top to see how it would look.

It was a perfect fit.

Almost immediately, my mind filled with all the worst-case scenarios. *What if I had to open the book during the interview? What if I had to read something from it?* I was already imagining a moment when my entire charade would be embarrassingly exposed for the online world to see.

Still, I decided to do the interview anyway.

The next day I showed up to the interview and proudly held up my book cover, fitted carefully on top of a worn copy of *Made to Stick*. I made it through the interview without my secret being exposed.

Many years (and interviews) later, I realized just how silly my concern had been. No one ever asks you to read from a business book during an interview. And no one, from a brief look, can tell that the interior of a book doesn't match the dust jacket anyway.

Of course, at the time I didn't know any of that and my problem felt monumental. Looking back, the "secret" to surviving that situation was self-confidence. The kind of self-confidence I had been sorely lacking nearly a decade earlier when I had what I not-so-fondly remember as the worst meeting of my life.

HOW TO FAIL MISERABLY AT SELLING YOUR IDEA

The year was 1998 and I had an idea that I thought was going to change the fine dining industry. At the time, very few restaurants had a website and so I had come up with an idea to use the Internet to bring these restaurants into the 21st century (literally, since it was still two years until the year 2000!).[1]

My business model consisted of services (getting restaurants to pay me to build their websites) and media (creating an online directory of websites that would become the place for anyone to find a restaurant).

To start, I registered the domain name *www.dc-restaurants. com* for my directory and then started my efforts by going door to door in a part of Washington, D.C. called Georgetown to try and convince restaurant owners to pay me $200 to build their website. Everyone asked me the same question: "Why would any restaurant need a website?" It was, after all, still 1998.

After more than a dozen rejections, I decided to go to one restaurant and offer to build their website for free just so I could pretend I had a paying client and entice other restaurant owners to give me a chance. After I built that site, I listed it on my directory along with the handful of DC area restaurants who already had websites that I had found online. Then I visited a few more restaurants. Even *that* didn't work.

As a last-ditch effort before giving up, I had an idea.

What if I could convince the dominant Internet provider at the time to list my directory and drive traffic to it? Then I could show the restaurant owners how many people were visiting my site and all the potential customers they were missing. It seemed like the perfect plan to convert those skeptical restauranteurs.

Part of what inspired that plan was the convenient fact that the headquarters of America's biggest Internet provider at the time happened to be right down the road from where I lived. After several calls, I managed to get a meeting with one of their regional directors.

A few weeks later, I walked into the lobby of the provider, which was already better known by its acronym: AOL. My big meeting started with some quick small talk, after which the director listened to my description of *www.dc-restaurants.com* patiently. I talked about the vision for the site. I talked about what I wanted to do for restaurant owners. I talked about how *sure* I was that AOL users would be very interested in finding restaurants online.

After quietly listening to me ramble on for about ten minutes, he said politely, "I understand what we can do for you. What can *you* do for us?"

Silence.

I didn't say anything. I didn't invent anything. I didn't even move. I just sat there. I didn't have an answer because I didn't have enough confidence to recall all the work I had done before.

Looking back, I realize there were plenty of things I *could* have said.

I could have mentioned the research I had seen about how more and more consumers were looking online for restaurants but that there was no directory of restaurants in our area yet. I could have told him about the few successful directories like mine that I had found in other cities which seemed to be thriving. I could have even told him about how I had researched AOL and knew they didn't have a directory like this one already.

Unfortunately, none of those facts came to mind, because I was too nervous. I failed because I didn't have the confidence or knowledge to be able to come up with a good answer to his reasonable question in the moment when I needed it.

After what seemed like an eternity, I finally said I would think about it and get back to him. I quietly thanked him for his time and escaped the room as quickly as I could. That was officially the worst business meeting of my life.

It would be easy for me to excuse my lack of confidence as a natural result of my age and inexperience. I used to think that if I had just been older and more experienced, perhaps I could have succeeded in that meeting.

Yet it seems like everywhere we look today, there are entrepreneurs who start billion-dollar overvalued "unicorn" companies and make the rest of us feel like underachievers, no matter how old we are.

Is it possible that some people just seem to earn their self-confidence faster than others? And if so, what do they know that everyone else doesn't?

THE POMEGRANATE PRINCIPLE

The answer comes from a fact you will quickly discover if you ever happen to search the Internet for advice on how to deseed a pomegranate. On the Internet, everyone seems to have a theory for the correct way to do this frustrating task.

The only thing all these self-declared experts agree on is the *wrong* way: slicing it in half and picking out the seeds individually. Instead, one popular video suggests cutting it in half and whacking the back of each half with a wooden spoon (highly entertaining but messy). Another illustrates how you could cut it into sixths and slowly peel it apart (precise but hard to do exactly right).

Finding divergent advice like this online is something we encounter often. The challenge is knowing which advice to follow.

. . . .

The Pomegranate Principle: In a world filled with conflicting advice, the ultimate skill is building and learning to trust your own intuition.

. . . .

Intuition can seem like an example of a big complex thing that is hard to intentionally improve. It isn't.

The truth is, intuition is built from the tiny observations that we all make every day. When you get a "gut feeling," it is an example of your brain using a memory from your past to help explain the present. Scientists call this *pattern matching* and human brains are great at it.

That's why it pays to focus on the details—no matter how small or insignificant. What if tiny little "life hacks," like learning how to deseed a pomegranate, were the real secret to improving your intuition?

Life hacks like using club soda to soak up a red wine stain. Or turning on a seat heater to keep takeout food warm in your car. Or rubbing a walnut on damaged wood furniture.

In *Always Eat Left Handed*, you will read about fifteen simple but useful ideas like these. To organize them, the book is divided into four parts.

The first part is called **Think Better**. It is all about encouraging you to be more observant, invest in yourself and how to be resilient after failure. The second part is **Work Better** and focuses on how to succeed in the professional workplace. You will learn about why it matters to have professional empathy and integrity, and why job descriptions and being on time are both overrated.

After that, the third part of the book is all about how to **Communicate Better** and offers a deeper look at the backstory behind my illogical disgust for cauliflower, why you should interrupt often and the power of simplifying and telling better stories. Finally, the fourth part includes ideas for how to **Connect Better**, including the unexpected benefits of cross-dressing and why you might *want* people to steal your ideas.

Each of the secrets is shared through the lens of a personal story, with minimal buzzwords and told as briefly as I could make it. For each, you will also get real actionable advice for how to put that idea to work in your personal or professional life, and why it matters.

When you are left handed, you are forced to see the world just a bit differently than other people. Regular everyday items like scissors or can openers just don't work for you.

Being left handed means you have to get better at finding your own solutions to life's tiny problems. That is a mentality we can all embrace, no matter which hand we happen to prefer.

So let's get started learning how to do it.

PART I

THINK BETTER

CHAPTER 2

Be Forgetful

THE SECRET: FIND YOUR RESILIENCE

THE FIRST TIME I HAD BREAKFAST WITH TIM FERRISS, HE WAS A GUY about to launch a book that had been rejected by 26 publishers.

We first connected through an email he sent saying he was a reader of my blog and asking to have breakfast together at the SXSW Festival in Austin, Texas (which he knew I was speaking at). Amidst the chaos of that event, we found a window to have breakfast at the Hilton hotel across the street from the madhouse of the Convention Center.

That morning he was peppering me with questions about marketing and blogging and sharing his ideas for promoting his soon-to-be-released book.

A few months later, his book called *The 4-Hour Workweek* came out and performed better than anyone predicted. It catapulted to become a #1 bestseller and in the years since has sold more than 1 million copies.

The second time we had breakfast together, he had stayed the night at our house and we were talking about his unlikely rise to fame and what he was going to do next. That day, I remember admiring how he was able to see past his continual failures and achieve something great.

We love to hear stories like this: people fighting past their early failures to achieve big success.

British inventor James Dyson, the creator of the best-selling line of premium vacuum cleaners, famously failed in designing the proper level of suction for his cyclone-powered vacuum more than *five thousand* times before finally getting it right.[2]

When Harry Potter series creator J.K. Rowling was writing the first Harry Potter book, she was a single mother on welfare writing her book from cafes in Edinburgh, Scotland. Her manuscript was also rejected by multiple publishers before one finally took a chance on her.

The stories of successful people seem filled with plenty of failures and rejections like these along the way … but there is another side of these stories that you rarely hear about.

WHAT THEY DON'T TELL YOU ABOUT FAILING

These big celebrated failures unfold over months and sometimes even years. They are memorable because of their duration and severity.

. . . .

> In real life, most of the failures you will have are not the sort of thing you will want to celebrate ... or even admit.

. . . .

What about the small *daily* failures that we have far more often? Failures like inadvertently posting that photo to Instagram without making sure there wasn't something embarrassing in the background. Or accidentally missing a deadline for work. Or not having the answer to a question you should have known.

These are the tiny embarrassing failures that weigh on our minds in the short term. When it comes to building your resilience overall, the real question is how can you train yourself to consistently overcome these types of setbacks, forget about them and move forward?

To answer that question, consider the extreme example of people who manage to survive in disastrous situations.

HOW TO SURVIVE DISASTER

When faced with a life-threatening moment, adventure writer Laurence Gonzales estimates that about 90% of people freeze or panic. What makes the other 10% maintain their calm and ultimately survive?

Gonzales explores this fascinating question in his book *Deep Survival: Who Lives, Who Dies, And Why*. The thing that sets survivors apart, according to Gonzales, is that "they immediately begin to recognize, acknowledge, and even accept the reality of their situation. They move through denial, anger, bargaining, depression, and acceptance very rapidly."

There is plenty of science to support this idea that the ability to be resilient and overcome adversity has a lot to do with how quickly you can accept the reality of a situation instead of dwelling on what could or should have happened instead.

THE ART OF CALM

Beyond acceptance, the next step toward real resilience is finding a way to remain calm. Gonzales also tells the story of interviewing former NASA psychologist Ephimia Morphew-Lu about the curious case of several scuba divers who had drowned despite having air in their tanks and working regulators.

Morphew, the founder of the *Journal of Human*

Performance in Extreme Environments, shared that after extensive study, researchers had finally concluded that the deaths were a result of an uncontrollable feeling of suffocation that some people feel when their mouths are covered.

This led victims to make the unintentionally suicidal choice to uncover their mouth and nose far under water and drown.

Panic literally killed the scuba divers.[3]

Being calmer in the face of adversity may not have such life and death implications—but when you add this skill to the ability to accept a situation and move on, you can become more resilient yourself in the face of almost any failure ... no matter how extreme.

HOW TO BE MORE RESILIENT

TIP #1 - SHIFT YOUR EXPLANATORY STYLE

Martin Seligman is a psychologist who is sometimes described as the "father of positive thinking" thanks to his lifelong mission to study, teach, and write about the relationship between optimism and pessimism and why people choose one or the other.

In his national bestseller *Learned Optimism,* he describes

one of the key differences between people who bounce back from adversity and those who don't in terms of their "explanatory style"—a term he uses to describe the way in which a person tends to explain situations in their mind.

If you challenged a group of people to draw a cat, for example, a person with a negative, pessimistic explanatory style might say or think "I can't draw anything," while a positive, resilient person might say "I'm not great at drawing a cat, but I *can* draw an amazing house."

Shifting your explanatory style to be positive and optimistic is within your control to do—and can have a big impact on your future success.

TIP #2 – Be Low Maintenance

When someone has a lot of unreasonable demands or requires constant attention, they are labeled as "high maintenance." In the real world, unless you happen to be a highly-paid pop music star, it usually pays to be the opposite. Sometimes when someone treats you dismissively or without the respect you think you deserve, it is not about you.

Feeling overwhelmed can make us all behave badly or slight someone without intending to. If someone doesn't return your message, choose to follow up with kindness instead of accusations. Most of us are just doing the best we can and many times the thing *you* need just won't be at the top of someone else's to do list. Get over it and try instead to have more empathy for someone else's situation.

TIP #3 – DON'T MENTION IT (FOR REAL)

When you hold a grudge or dwell on a string of failures, the usual way that it comes up over time is through minor comments or remarks mentioning it in passing that demonstrate how much you have *not* forgotten about it and have not moved on. To fight against that, make a mental commitment that once you have publicly shared that you are "over it"—you will not mention "it" anymore—even in small side comments.

This commitment is the ultimate self-fulfilling prophecy. In other words, once you make the mental commitment to not mention it, you will end up really getting over it much more quickly. Of course, this doesn't mean avoiding a problem—so if something is unresolved, you need to face it head on first ... *then* you can actually move on and not mention it.

CHAPTER 3

Start Smoking

THE SECRET: CONTROL YOUR DESTINY

When I first moved to Australia, the best way I found to get to know my fellow workers was to join them on the several smoking breaks many of them took throughout the day.

I had never been a smoker, but I decided to give it a try despite all the health concerns. As I did, I made a promise to myself that after a month, no matter what, I would stop.

So I started smoking—and enjoyed it. For that month, every day I would go out with my new colleagues and we had a low pressure moment during the day to just hang out—the more modern equivalent of the old water cooler conversations.

After a month I stopped smoking, but kept going out for those smoking breaks. Looking back I know that smoking helped me build some professional relationships because it gave me a time to socialize outside of the usual work day. You might be wondering why I couldn't have done that without ever smoking.

It is easy to cave to peer pressure and do something like smoking because you are pressured to do it or would feel excluded if you didn't. Making your own choice (whether to start smoking, or to stop) is much harder.

Is smoking dangerous and can it kill you? Of course. So is having a poisonous snake for a pet—but some crazy people do that, too. The problem with smoking isn't having the occasional cigarette. The problem is how easy it is to become addicted.

Smoking worked for me because I *chose* to start so I had a reason to join those smoking breaks, and I *chose* to stop because I knew I wasn't going to let myself get addicted.

As you probably already figured out, this secret isn't really about starting to smoke at all. It is about making symbolic choices, though they sometimes may be risky, to control your own destiny.

WHY YOU SHOULD PICK THE WINDOW SEAT

How does this idea translate to doing things other than smoking a product which can give you cancer? Symbolic choices don't always need to be this life-threatening. They can even come from something as simple as choosing where to sit on a flight.

When CNN ran a poll asking business travelers whether they preferred the window seat or the aisle, the vast majority tended to prefer the convenience of the aisle seat.

When you sit in an aisle seat, it is more efficient and takes less time to get off the plane when it lands. It is much easier to go to the bathroom. It is more convenient to be served any meal or drinks. And you can access any items stored in the overhead bins easily. No wonder it is far more popular among business travelers.

Except me. I always choose the window seat.

IT'S NOT ABOUT THE VIEW

Sure, I love the view—but the window seat offers more than that. In a closed environment, having the window seat offers you just a little control over your in-flight experience.

In the window seat, you choose whether to keep the window shade open or closed. When you need to go to the bathroom (if you do), everyone else gets up to let you out. If you don't and choose to stay in your seat for the whole flight, no one disturbs you.

Where you choose to sit on the plane (assuming you have a choice!) can change your experience of traveling. This same principle applies to much more than picking a seat for a flight.

How many situations are you just along for the ride but not really in control? It can be easy to feel this way professionally and sometimes even personally as well.

. . . .

Being empowered is a choice that we all must make, even if it comes in the smallest seemingly insignificant of places ... like picking the window seat on a flight.

. . . .

Ultimately, it comes down to controlling your own destiny ... a phrase that we commonly hear from the world of athletics as well.

CHAMPIONS DON'T LOSE THEIR WAY FORWARD

In every sport that features championships, there are generally two ways to make it to the final rounds of competition. You can beat the teams that you need to beat and *earn* your spot. That's the best way. But then, there's the other way. You can hope that another team loses, back into a spot and *accidentally* make it by default.

Coaches talk about that in terms of controlling your own destiny. Winning teams earn that control. If they win, they get in. Outside of the sports world, the importance of controlling your own destiny can be equally important. In surveys of workplace cultures, empowerment always ranks highly as something the best workplaces always offer to employees. For many entrepreneurs, this can be a primary motivation for starting their own businesses as well.

HOW TO CONTROL YOUR DESTINY

TIP #1 - CHOOSE TO LEAD INSTEAD OF FOLLOW

Controlling your own destiny from the back seat is tough. Sometimes you have the role you have, and there's no way around it. Other times, however, there is an element of choice. When I got my first job in Australia, it was a short three-week gig doing programming, and halfway into the project, I realized the real reason they hired me: the project was behind because of bad management. What they really needed was a new project manager. So I started doing that job without being asked. A week later I was officially hired full-time to do it. Sometimes the chance to lead is something that isn't given to you—but rather something that depends upon your own initiative.

TIP #2 - Embrace Your Fidgeting

In school, we are told that being easily distracted is not a good thing. Many kids take medication to control their impulses at school and be less "fidgety." Outside of school, though, the fidgeting may actually serve an important purpose. Learning to embrace your fidgeting—whether it is something like playing with a pencil or shaking your leg (or any other annoying habit for the people around you) can offer an unexpected way to help you focus. So buy little gadgets like "fidget cubes" or start doodling on conference calls, or find another way to *enable* your fidgeting rather than trying to bury it or medicate it. That is creative energy and learning to tap into it in the right way can pay off huge dividends.

TIP #3 - Walk Away

Several years ago the BBC aired a documentary about the inhumane working conditions in multiple factories in China that were building iPhones and iPads for Apple.[4] The program described long working hours, cramped living quarters and demanding bosses. What struck me, though, was a moment in the piece where a worker talked about the overwhelming sense of hopelessness that came from working in an assembly line job with the same robotic schedule fourteen hours a day, six days a week. It was the lack of free will that was destroying his will to survive and even causing him to contemplate suicide. Most of us will thankfully never have to endure a job situation like that, but sometimes our jobs or lives might *feel* like an endless loop. If that feeling lasts for too long, you have an option that most desperate Chinese factory workers don't. You can walk away and start something new.

CHAPTER 4

REINVENT YOUR PLAYLIST

THE SECRET: OVERSPEND ON YOURSELF

OVER THE PAST FIVE YEARS, I HAVE PROBABLY PURCHASED MORE than five hundred books. That's an average of about two per week, but my buying is rarely that steady. Instead, I buy in bursts that usually coincide with some new project or book I am working on.

For me, starting something new inspires me to buy books. But when you buy that many books, there are a couple of inconvenient facts that you are forced to confront. The first is that you will quickly run out of space to keep all those books. The second is that it becomes nearly impossible to read all of them. In my case, the end result is that I'm routinely buying some books that I will *never* read and probably end up reselling or donating within a year.

Why would anyone buy books they don't read? It may seem odd but think about the last five non-school-related books you've bought (not counting this one!). Maybe you can't even remember them. But if you can, then how many of them have you actually read cover to cover?

People buy books they don't read all the time, they just don't usually admit it. Sometimes it is because they like the cover. Often it is with the best intentions to read them, but then life gets in the way and time gets short.

I see books as an investment, rather than a guilt-inducing reminder of unfinished homework.

I buy them for the ideas buried inside that I hope will emerge at the right moment to help me solve a challenge I have or change my thinking about a topic. And sometimes that moment never comes. Other times, it comes merely from reading the first few chapters of a book and never finishing the rest. I never put pressure on myself to finish every book I start.

WHY READING BOOKS IS LIKE BUILDING A PLAYLIST

Instead, I focus on finding the most valuable ideas that I can apply to my work or that change the way I think. Then I take those ideas and assemble them into my own "playlist" where I combine them together and start to make connections between them.

If you think about it, this is not so different from how most of us build a playlist for listening to music or watching videos online. We assemble songs, shows or ideas into groups and then enjoy them together.

I realize many teachers would disagree with this playlist-inspired advice for reading books (and sometimes not finishing them).

. . . .

I believe your time is too valuable to waste finishing a book you don't enjoy or find useful.

. . . .

Not every book you're going to read will be *worth* finishing, and that's okay. Finally admitting this fact to yourself can be a huge source of mental relief. When you do give yourself this freedom, you will find that you enjoy the books that you do finish so much more—and you will probably read more books as a result.

Of course, I realize that the fact that I happen to overspend on books is probably not surprising since I am a writer. What about people who find their success and career in something else?

SPEND LIKE A MILLIONAIRE SELF-HELP GURU

A few years ago, I was invited to attend an exclusive event with one hundred high-profile speakers, leadership coaches, entrepreneurs and self-help gurus. Among the participants were best-selling authors and influencers who had worked directly with some of the biggest names in the personal development space, from Gretchen Rubin to Deepak Chopra.

As the event went on, I listened hungrily for the insights they all shared to explain their many successes. They talked about revenue models and presentation styles. They shared everything from selling techniques to creating information products that people couldn't wait to buy. One conversation, in particular, stood out. The host of the event posed a simple question to the group: How much do you spend in an average year on personal development?

The answers amazed me.

Almost everyone admitted to spending well over $10,000 a year on this ... and several said they spent *more* than $100,000 a year! This included everything from videos to books to hiring personal coaches to attending exclusive events.

Even more significantly, many of them attributed their current success to their willingness to take the money they were making earlier in their careers and reinvest it in themselves.

Listening to these highly successful people—many of whom were easily making over a million dollars a year—the results of overspending on themselves seemed apparent. Even though my more modest version of this at the time just involved buying several hundred books a year, I left inspired to do more than that.

It is easy to think of investing in yourself as something you may have already done in order to earn a college degree or an MBA (whether you had to pay for it yourself or not). Earning a degree is just the start—and for some highly successful and unconventional people, it may even be a traditional step they end up skipping. The goal isn't a piece of paper, it's becoming a better and smarter person, and there are many ways to spend on that.

A QUICK WORD OF CAUTION ...

Before I share some tips on how to do this, I should offer a quick word of caution. My advice to "overspend" on yourself doesn't mean you should put yourself deeply into debt or chase too many opportunities you can't afford. Take risks when you can, be strategic, but also have patience. When you are building a career, there are some experiences you have to earn with time—and the money to afford them may come with time as well.

HOW TO OVERSPEND ON YOURSELF

TIP #1 - Focus on What You're Great At

Growing up, we tend to focus on our weakest areas and try to bring them up to par. Failing math? Go find a math tutor. In the real world, successful people do the opposite: they try to get even better at what they are *already* great at.

For example, last year I spent more than $20,000 on professional training and coaching for myself to become a better keynote speaker and performer *while* I was teaching a class on public speaking and storytelling to master's level students at Georgetown University.

As I told my students at the time, you are never too good to get better. Today I charge $25,000 to deliver a keynote speech.

TIP #2 - Invest in Experiences, Not Stuff

You will never regret the money you spend to have an amazing experience.

In August 2012, I was thinking about starting my own company and money was tight, but the London Olympics had just started and I was desperate to go. I had already been to three Summer Olympic Games (Atlanta, Sydney, and Beijing) and I couldn't imagine missing this one when it was a mere six-hour flight from my home in Washington, DC.

So I booked a last-minute ticket with my eight-year-old son and we went for a weekend. To fund the trip (since it was before my speaking career took off), I skipped getting a new car and kept driving my twelve-year-old car for another year. Four years later, we could afford it, and our whole family went to Brazil for the Games.

The Olympics are now a tradition for us every four years and one that I know my entire family will never forget.

TIP #3 - Trade What You Have

Early in your career, you will probably have more time than money. Use that to your advantage to volunteer to be part of events or experiences that can help you learn something new or expand your network. Start by reaching out to visionary people you admire and craft an offer to help them in a way that would be beneficial to them. Do your research to uncover what that might be. You will be surprised at how many of them will respond to a well thought out unsolicited offer to help from someone hungry for experience and ready to work for it.

CHAPTER 5

LEARN TO YODEL

THE SECRET: ACQUIRE "USELESS" KNOWLEDGE

I REMEMBER ATTENDING A PERFORMANCE OF SHAKESPEARE'S *Twelfth Night* at the Folger Theater, one of the most famous Shakespearean theaters in the world. The play is a love story gone wrong—the tale of a young shipwrecked woman named Viola who must pretend to be a man to get work as a servant and then accidentally falls in love with the man she serves, a music-loving Duke named Orsino.

The play's most famous line—"if music be the food of love, play on"—describes the passion Orsino has for music and is also the inspiration for the music-filled production I watched that day. The show had a live keyboard player, banjo, guitar, drums and singing to accompany the traditional Shakespearean dialogue.

The most memorable moment of the production came about halfway through when the character Viola enters, sits on a chair in the middle of the stage and starts playing the cello as the love triangle of the story plays out in the scene around her. It was the sort of moment that happens often in the world of the arts. Characters are created around the skills and personalities of the actors who play them.

Emily Trask, the actress who played Viola, is also a trained cellist. According to her entertaining bio, she has also studied dance, can swing from a trapeze, and knows how to yodel. You could easily argue that none of these talents are critical to becoming an actress. Independently, each may seem like a fairly useless skill.

Yet when it came to landing the coveted leading role of Viola in this renowned production of *Twelfth Night* at the Folger, playing the cello became very useful indeed. Her ability to yodel might have even helped her get the casting call in the first place.

The point is, the story of Emily Trask is a perfect illustration of how acquiring *useless* knowledge can turn out to be surprisingly *useful* over time.

A FATEFUL NIGHT AT THE THEATER

Steve Jobs is famous for many things. When he passed away, the tributes to his legacy of products and ideas seemed never-ending. Admirers praised his uncompromising vision, his legendary presentation skills and his gift for simplifying big technical challenges into digestible chunks. What received much less attention was his habit of acquiring useless knowledge.

Like when he dropped out of college and decided to take a calligraphy class to learn about typefaces and print graphic design – which eventually led to the Macintosh being the first computer to have built-in fonts.

Or when he traveled to India to learn about meditation and practice Zen Buddhism – which inspired his belief in the necessity for design to be simple.

The story of Steve Jobs isn't only a story about a visionary inventor. It is also a story of a man thirsty for knowledge about the world and who often managed to apply that knowledge in powerful ways.

There are plenty of other famous people with unique skills and passions as well. Here are a few:

FAMOUS PERSON	WHAT THEY DO
Taylor Swift	… makes snow globes and jams
Nick Offerman	… loves woodworking
Seth Meyers	… has written comic books
Mila Kunis	… plays World of Warcraft
Neil Patrick Harris	… is an avid magician
Beyoncé	… is a painter and art collector

What the stories of Steve Jobs, Emily Trask and all these other famous people and their quirky skills illustrate is an underappreciated truth about acquiring so-called useless knowledge: it can often help you think differently than anyone else or stand out in unexpected ways.

HOW TO ACQUIRE KNOWLEDGE

TIP #1 - ASK MORE QUESTIONS

One of my favorite parts of being a dad is hearing all kinds of questions from my kids about everything from why they speak Portuguese in Brazil to why motorcycles don't have seatbelts. From my University students, I sadly get far fewer questions. As we get older, there are many reasons our questions become less frequent. Sometimes we are afraid to appear foolish. Sometimes we mistakenly think the information we need will appear when we need it (or be a Google search away). Other times we just might not know what we don't know. It doesn't have to be like this. The first step in acquiring useless knowledge is *choosing* to ask more questions about unfamiliar topics. The closely related second step is to *listen* to the answers.

TIP #2 - BUY UNFAMILIAR MAGAZINES

A few years ago when I was traveling through South Africa, I picked up a magazine called *Farmer's Weekly*, intended for commercial farmers. One of the stories in the issue focused on something the author called the "Amish Paradox," which refers to the Amish practice of rotating crops and avoiding chemical fertilizers engineered for commercial farms to help them grow bigger fruit and vegetables in less time. Instead, the Amish grow smaller produce more slowly and rotate crops more deliberately to keep their land and soil healthier.

As a result, their land remains fertile longer. Despite not working in farming, the broader message I took away from that article was that sometimes you need to give up short-term gains to focus on the long-term goal instead ... and it came from a magazine that most people would have assumed to be useless to anyone not working in the farming industry.

TIP #3 - MAXIMIZE YOUR COUCH TIME

Self-help books will never tell you to spend more time on your couch. Yet there is a powerful archive of amazing learning you can access straight from your couch through great documentary films, or podcasts, or TED Talks or random YouTube videos on random topics (like deseeding a pomegranate!). Enjoy your couch time, and feel free to increase it … as long as you're maximizing it by engaging your brain. If, however, you end up binge-watching old seasons of "Real Housewives" episodes, more couch time is not helping you. Ignore this tip and get off your couch to go do something else. *Right now.*

PART II

WORK BETTER

CHAPTER 6

Ignore Your Job

THE SECRET: DELIVER WHAT THEY DON'T ASK FOR

MOST PEOPLE WRITING A JOB DESCRIPTION START WITH THE SAME sad first steps: a Google search followed by lots of cutting and pasting. The reason is simple: writing a job description is hard. Even people who spend all day recruiting and interviewing job candidates generally hate writing job descriptions. It's hard to fit everything in. Yet no matter how long or detailed a job listing seems, one thing has always been true ... no one ever hired anyone hoping they would ONLY do what was listed in their job description.

. . . .

Your job description is not a finish line, it is a starting line.

. . . .

Yes, you do need to do your job. And whether that "job" involves working for someone else, or even launching your own startup, there are bound to be some things you don't enjoy doing or think you are overqualified for.

The biggest chances you will have to prove yourself hardly ever fit into the thin confines of your job description. Instead, they will challenge you to do something you never imagined you would need to do. Something like standing very, very still for an extended period.

THE TIME I (SORT OF) MET AL GORE

Several years ago I had the chance to attend the first edition of a now annual event called the Future of Storytelling. It was an elite audience and I was there with the CEO of the company I was working for at the time to help him present on the art of storytelling. I had worked for weeks on learning his presentation and he had promised to give me the chance to present a few slides alongside him for the first time.

Our session was hosted in a small room with an A-list participant list of only about twenty-five people, including former U.S. Vice President Al Gore. Unfortunately, the projector available in the room was not working and my CEO had a highly visual presentation with lots of slides.

The only improvised solution we had was for him to present directly from his laptop. That could work because of the small size of the room … but there was another problem.

We were minutes away from our scheduled start time and there was no chair or table high enough to place the laptop on so most people could see it.

In an instant, my "job" was clear. I would have to hold his laptop up for forty-five minutes so he could present. Unfortunately, that would make co-presenting awkward and probably impossible ... and so my big chance to present had vanished.

Rather than focusing on myself, though, I did what I had to do to make that presentation work. At the time, I was disappointed. Looking back, I realized the lesson in humility that I also learned that day. You're never too important to do what it takes to get the job done ... even if it means posing as a human table for forty-five minutes.

BRINGING LATTES TO AMERICA

One of the best examples of ignoring a job description comes from the founding story of a brand many of us interact with daily. In the 1970s, a salesman named Howard Schultz was leading a team at a Swedish company selling housewares when he got an unusually large order for drip coffeemakers. The order piqued his curiosity and he decided to travel to Seattle to meet with the tiny coffee shop owners who had placed the order—Gerald Baldwin and Gordon Bowker.

Over the course of the next year, Schultz steadily worked to convince them both to hire him as the director of marketing, and finally in 1982 he moved to Seattle and joined the team at the small coffee shop known as Starbucks. Only a year after starting, Schultz visited Italy on what has now become part of the legend of the founding of Starbucks. It was there he realized that coffee shops could be meeting points for a community and that the idea of Italian-style coffee drinks like the latte and espresso might be popular in the U.S. as well.

Inspired, he came back to Seattle and convinced the founders to start selling those drinks. He felt the future of the brand could be huge, but the owners worried that expanding would mean losing the individuality of Starbucks, so Schultz left in 1986 to start his own coffee chain called Il Giornale. A year later Baldwin and Bowker put the Starbucks brand up for sale and Schultz immediately got a loan to buy it.[5]

The story of Schultz and his outsized vision for that tiny chain of coffee shops in Seattle is one that some of you might have heard before. Starbucks is clearly a huge success story, with more than 21,000 stores in 65 countries and a current market value of more than $70 billion. Yet if you look at Schultz's unlikely path toward CEO of one of the world's most valuable brands, there is a clear pattern of never being constrained by his job title.

When he was leading a sales team, he took a pay cut for half his salary at the time to join Starbucks. When he was leading marketing for Starbucks, he wanted to expand rapidly and ended up leaving to become an entrepreneur and start his own coffee shop. And when he came back to buy the brand, he promised his investors he would open at least 100 new stores in his first five years of business (which he did easily).

You might look at a successful entrepreneur like Schultz and think that his story is unique, but the lessons behind it are ones you can use to propel your own career and life forward too. He refused to be defined by his job title at any point in his career, no matter how good the job might have been. You don't have to start a multibillion-dollar company to have that same mindset. It all starts with choosing to be more than the title on your business card and thinking beyond your role.

HOW TO DELIVER WHAT THEY DIDN'T ASK

TIP #1 - UNDERSTAND THE REAL NEED

There are usually two sides to a task that someone asks you to do: the task itself and the underlying need behind it. Professional organizational consultants, for example, understand that often they will be called by someone who is suffering from feeling overloaded by the things that they own. The solution, in that person's mind, is to get a better organizational system to store their stuff.

What great organizers understand, though, is that usually the problem is only *partially* based on a lack of organization. Instead, what people really need is to form new *habits* along with a new organizational system. The key to getting organized is training yourself to stick to a system that you develop—otherwise, that overwhelming feeling will just come back when the disarray inevitably builds up again.

TIP #2 - MAKE IT BETTER

Improving on something before delivering it is a key element of going above and beyond what is asked. There will be plenty of times in your career when you are asked to just "get it done." I remember one such time when I was living in Australia and had been asked last minute to assist a visiting American colleague to organize her presentation to our Sydney office.

As part of helping review her slides, I changed the spelling of various words such as *color* into *colour* because the Aussies use British spelling conventions. She hadn't asked me to do it, but she noticed. Can you get in trouble for doing more than you're asked? Of course. Is it worth it? In my case, it was.

The next time an opportunity came along to collaborate with the U.S. office, she specifically offered me the first chance to work on it because I had demonstrated to her in that small moment that I would always be thinking about making something better instead of just doing what I was told to do.

TIP #3 - REWRITE YOUR JOB DESCRIPTION

People are hired based on job descriptions all the time out of necessity, but that doesn't mean a weak or incomplete description of your job should hold you back from doing your best work. Rather than wait for your performance review or some other scheduled moment for evaluating your performance, take some time and rewrite your job description *on purpose*.

Consider what you're doing that you shouldn't be, and what you would like to be doing *more* of in an ideal world. Then write it down on paper. The next time you do have a meeting to discuss your role, doing this will give you a clearer picture of how to direct the conversation. After all, the most qualified person to write your job description is you ... *after* you've already been doing the job.

CHAPTER 7

NEVER SERVE BURNT TOAST

THE SECRET: HAVE INTEGRITY WHEN NO ONE IS LOOKING

THERE WAS A TIME WHEN I THOUGHT MY JOB WAS TO DELIVER toast as quickly as possible.

I had just graduated from college and was working as a waiter in a popular downtown café in Washington, D.C. At the time I was holding down two jobs while I studied for my master's degree. Waiting tables was the one I loved. It involved more personal interaction with new people every day and was way more exciting than my other desk-bound job. I was also better at it.

At the time, I didn't realize just how much working in a restaurant would teach me about relating to people ... particularly angry ones. Specifically, I remember this one irate customer who taught me a lifelong lesson after I made a big mistake with her order.

MY TOUGHEST CUSTOMER

I never asked her name, but I can still picture her face. That morning she was clearly not having a good day. She was alone, on her phone talking about something that was clearly only important in Washington, D.C.—like an upcoming vote on some obscure bill that hardly anyone had ever heard of.

I guessed that she was a lobbyist. Not wanting to interrupt, I was watching her out of the corner of my eye while taking care of my other tables but had not gone up to take her order yet. That was my first mistake.

When she was finally off her call, she was already annoyed. "I've been sitting here for like half an hour!" she said. "Are you my waiter?"

I nodded and tried to be friendly. She seemed to warm up a bit and ordered an omelet with toast. Then she pulled some papers out of her bag and started to look over them.

I placed her order in the system. If I had the breakfast shift, many of the meals I served included toast. Every once in a while that toast would come out a little "extra crispy" on one side.

A common trick my fellow waiters and I used was to flip the toast over so the better-looking side was presented face-up. We assumed most people would never know the difference.

My annoyed lobbyist customer that day was not one of those people. I knew I had made my second and much bigger mistake the moment I put that toast down. She picked it up, turned it over and then she looked at me.

Not wanting to get yelled at, I quickly offered to get her a new plate of toast ... anticipating what she was about to say. Realizing that yelling at me probably wasn't a good use of her time, she instead asked me a question I will never forget: "If you knew it was burnt, why did you give it to me?"

It would have taken me an extra minute to wait for a different plate of toast and serve her non-burnt toast instead of just flipping one slice over. But I didn't.

As you can probably guess, I didn't get much of a tip on that meal.

What I remember more than that is the fact that I missed the chance to do what I knew was right instead of what I knew was easy. I missed a chance to have integrity when no one was looking over my shoulder and demanding it.

WHAT IF NO ONE IS LOOKING?

How many times in our lives do we get the chance to take the easy way out? More than we probably realize. Most of us don't go through life with security cameras watching our every move. And even if we did, choosing *not* to be lazy or selfish isn't always an easy thing to do.

Several months ago, I contracted with a small company and handyman to do some construction work. I asked him to start and paid my deposit. Just a day later, I was doing some research online and discovered that there was a special rebate offer on one of the materials that the contractor had recommended and we had already approved. I assumed he knew about it and planned to keep the rebate for himself.

Before I could ask about it, I got an unsolicited email about it from the contractor. The email shared a link to the rebate and promised that after he purchased the materials and received it, he planned to give me a credit for half of it. I wasn't expecting him to share any of it, much less tell me about it. Most contractors wouldn't.

His short-term choice to do business with integrity cost him half of the rebate—about $200. Yet I was so impressed with the experience, that I have told more than a dozen people about it and already helped him get at least two more large projects.

His choice to do business with integrity brought more referrals and trust.

HOW TO HAVE MORE INTEGRITY

TIP #1 - Share the Unexpected Truth

There are some truths we expect. You can't lie about the degree you earned in school or about where a product you are selling was made. But we don't often expect to hear someone *proactively* tell the truth—especially in a sales situation.

For example, we don't expect the mechanic to tell us how much he *actually* makes after he charges us for a job. What if he did? That kind of honesty would stand out—and it is the perfect example of the power of sharing the truth before anyone forces you to. When you can find the courage to share things that your competitors or other colleagues don't, then you can stand apart based on your unprompted honesty.

TIP #2 - DO WHAT YOU SAY YOU WILL DO

During conversation, most of us tend to make lots of promises. We promise we will introduce one person to another. We promise we will get back to someone on a request they shared. We set professional deadlines for ourselves. Integrity is doing what you say you will do—and this applies to even the most basic of promises.

When I suggest that I can make a connection for someone, I always do it. If I promise to share the name of a great book with someone after mentioning it, I make a point of sending a follow-up note with the name and a link to buy it. The point is, being "world class" at following up is one way to do what you say, and something any of us can get better at doing more routinely.

TIP #3 – Put Your Name on It

Unlike many other professors, when I give my students a writing assignment, I never give them a minimum required length. Instead, I ask them to give me a well-thought-out and well-written piece on the assigned topic—as long as they need for it to be. If they can address the topic of the week in a powerful and compelling way with one sentence, I invite them to do it.

The one thing I do insist upon, though, is that they put their name on it and publish their assignment publicly on our class blog. This transparency means every other student in the class can read it too—and I grade them publicly on a 1 to 5 scale through a comment on their post.

My reason for this is to underscore one of the most basic truths about the Internet: that everything you share online reflects your reputation. By putting their name on it, my students are making a promise that they stand behind their work, and that usually means they try harder to deliver great writing and thinking.

I'm still hoping one of them delivers that perfectly crafted one sentence response. So far, no one has.

CHAPTER 8

BE A CROSS-DRESSER

THE SECRET: LEARN EMPATHY

FRANK BAIRD HAD A CRAZY IDEA.

While working as a community advocate and family therapist in California with women and families broken apart by domestic abuse, he wanted to find a new way to create more visibility and dialogue around the cause. At a time when there were plenty of important causes competing for attention, Frank needed to create something that could simultaneously deliver shock value and generate empathy for the cause as well.

His concept was to create a march he called "Walk a Mile in Her Shoes" where he invited men to do exactly that by agreeing to wear bright red high heels and walk a mile.

Doing it, they would create a spectacle that no one could ignore, and bring awareness to this important cause in the process. The event was a big hit, generated lots of attention, and by 2017 more than 1,700 of these walks had been organized in local communities across the U.S.[6]

Today domestic abuse is a highly visible topic, with global concerts featuring stars like Beyoncé and major films like *Girl Rising* depicting stories of hope and change to bring education to more girls and women around the world and break the cycle of domestic abuse and lack of opportunities for women.

THE MYTH OF CROSS-DRESSING

The experience of a man walking in high heels creates empathy. It is also an example of cross-dressing—a term that has new meaning today.

We live in a time where a young celebrity like Jaden Smith will model traditionally women's clothing for Louis Vuitton. Facebook has already evolved from offering 71 profile options for gender to now making the choices unlimited.

All of this gender flux has the powerful side effect of creating more empathy between traditional gender boundaries and offering more empowerment for everyone. Adding to this effect is the rapid adoption of virtual reality.

HOW VIRTUAL EMPATHY WILL CHANGE THE WORLD

We can now *experience* what it is like to be a prisoner in solitary confinement or a teenager living in a refugee camp or even a cow being led to the slaughterhouse. These types of experiences are transformative and allow us to feel deeply the plight of another—and therefore have more empathy ourselves. They are the virtual equivalent of Frank's march in women's shoes.

Whether you build your own empathy through walking in high heels or donning a virtual reality mask, being able to see the world from a different perspective can bring you very unexpected but welcome results. As a doctor named Mark Siegler learned, empathy might even change the course of your career.[7]

THE $42-MILLION-DOLLAR QUESTION

It all started with a woman named Carolyn Bucksbaum who was having a difficult time getting doctors to listen to her ideas about what might be ailing her. This type of dysfunctional relationship between doctor and patient is sadly familiar.

When every patient walks in with pages of printouts from questionably authoritative websites offering everything from unverified data on rare conditions to information about too-good-to-be-true miracle cures, it can be hard for medical professionals to empathize.

Bucksbaum's story had a special significance, though, not because of her negative experience with her first skeptical doctor but because of her second doctor, Mark Siegler. Dr. Siegler took the time to listen to her theories and confirmed that, in fact, her self-diagnosis had turned out to be correct.

Bucksbaum was so impressed, she decided along with her husband that the type of empathetic bedside manner Dr. Siegler had used with them should be encouraged and taught more frequently.

They could also afford to do something about it. The Bucksbaums had made a small fortune building retail shopping malls and to give back, they decided to donate $42 million dollars for the creation of a new clinical center that would focus on teaching medical professionals how to have more empathy in communications with patients—an actual bedside manner school. The only requirement was that Dr. Mark Siegler had to be in charge.

HOW TO LEARN EMPATHY

TIP #1 - Imagine a Dramatic Backstory

When you are faced with someone who's behavior you don't understand in a professional or personal context, often it is because you can't imagine a situation where you yourself would act in such a way. To increase your ability to empathize, imagine a dramatic scenario wherein their behavior might be totally justified. Would you understand someone being short and rude to you on the phone if they had just spilled an entire cup of coffee on their desk? Probably.

The fact is, we don't often know the full backstories of most of the people we interact with or what they might have been going through at that exact moment. Creating that backstory in your own head, even if it is completely made up, can help you to not take any slights so personally and generally have more empathy for people whose actions you might otherwise struggle to understand.

TIP #2 - BEWARE OF UNINTENTIONAL INCENTIVES

Our behavior in many ways is ruled by the incentives that are around us. When call center staff are measured on spending as little time on the phone per call with a customer as possible, the predictable result is that they become rude, short, and eager to transfer a customer quickly instead of taking the time to solve their problem.

If you are given the direction in a new job that every hour you spend must be documented in some sort of complex timesheet system, you will be far less likely to help a colleague running a project that doesn't have a billable hour to "pay" for your time. At work, it is often the incentives we are *told* matter that cause us to act in selfish or uncollaborative ways.

If the incentives don't change, it can be almost impossible to change the behaviors that they are encouraging.

Tip #3 - Ask About Emotions

When we interact with one another, most of us are good at asking questions about things: *Where did you go? What did you do?* We are generally not as good at asking questions directly about emotions: *Why are you feeling sad? Are you angry?*

These questions reflect the mood and facial expressions you may be reading, but often we feel they cross a social boundary or may lead to unwanted answers and therefore we stay away from them. They seem too personal, particularly if asked at work. But sometimes just noticing and asking about emotions is the perfect way to encourage someone to open up and share a little more of how they are feeling. When you ask about feelings, you are immediately empathizing on a level that more general questions rarely break through.

The best way to build enough trust to get an honest answer is to share some of your own emotions and be a bit vulnerable yourself. The more you can share openly, the more likely it is you will get people to open up to you. And if you do get an answer, trying your best to listen with empathy can help you build deeper, more trusted relationships with the people around you—because you took the time to ask them about something important and then actually took the time to *listen* to the answer.

CHAPTER 9

PROCRASTINATE MORE

THE SECRET: BE IN TIME INSTEAD OF ON TIME

JAMES BOND IS NEVER ON TIME.

In fact, that's what makes him so good at what he does. He arrives at the last minute just as the bomb is about to explode or the girl is about to get shot, and he manages to save the day. Bond, like any great action hero, doesn't go through his day following Google calendar reminders on his phone. His phone (I'm guessing) probably doesn't even have them. Instead, he reacts to the situation, and he's never late. Bond is not *on time*, he's always *in time*.

What's the difference?

Being *on time* usually means following a pre-scripted schedule for your day. You can be on time for an interview or on time for a lunch date—and that is important. Showing up when you say you will is a sign of integrity.

Being *in time*, however, is all about choosing the right time to do something.

. . . .

Being in time is all about understanding the moment instead of blindly following the clock.

. . . .

People who have mastered the art of being in time show up exactly when they are needed most, deliver solutions that people don't expect and are adept at identifying moments of opportunity, no matter how fleeting they might be.

You hear a lot of people telling you to be punctual, but if being in time is so valuable, you might wonder how come no one ever teaches you how to do that?

There is no class on how to procrastinate till the last minute and then deliver something awesome on a short timeline right when it is needed most.

But maybe there should be.

THE PROBLEM WITH "JUST-IN-CASE" EDUCATION

Since early in grade school, our education is very infrequently connected directly to the world around us. Much of this education is "just in case"—things that we learn either because of tradition or the mistaken belief that that one day we may need to know them or choose a profession that uses them.

Calculus, the history of Mesopotamia, how to spot iambic pentameter ... these are all pieces of knowledge that you may or may not use through the course of your life. Sadly, if a moment arises in the future where you *did* need to know about any of those topics, chances are you wouldn't remember enough of what you learned years ago in order for it to be useful anyway.

As you get older, the problem gets even more pronounced. The typical MBA program lasts two years, during which time every aspect of business is taught through courses on leadership, finance, accounting, marketing, and human resources. The predictable problem is many of the students won't use the lessons they learn in an MBA program until years later in their careers, if ever.

The fundamental flaw with all this just-in-case education is that no one remembers things forever. Wouldn't it be better to teach the students the skills they need in the moment they need them?

Most academics agree that the solution is to give people more "just-in-time" education—either delivered through professional training or real-life internships or anything else that relates directly to what they need to know now.[8] Training like that is more useful, helps focus on solving real challenges, and better prepares each of us to succeed in the real world.

WHY TIMING REALLY IS EVERYTHING

This problem in traditional education underscores how little we tend to focus on being in time with our learning instead of on time. Of course, timing is vital to get right for far more than education.

Product launches, hiring decisions, and even the moments when you meet the right people (or don't) all depend on timing. In almost every case, there is no single road map of time that you can point to and say there is a perfect time for a particular event to occur.

What if constantly checking the clock on your phone or fitness tracker turns out to be the *least* useful way to think about time? Instead, when you forget about the clock, it frees your mind to think about being *in time* for experiences instead of mindlessly going through your daily schedule stressing about everything.

One secret to help you do this more effectively is to consider the impact organization may be having on your timing throughout the day. When you are about to leave your house, do you madly scramble to find your keys or your phone or a portable charger?

These are all time wasters that can throw off your timing even though you think you are leaving in time. Rather than lose time in that last critical moment, change your organizational system to avoid this mad scramble in the first place.

Part of being in time is knowing where to find the things that you need at the moment you need them. Remember when James Bond is diffusing a bomb, he always knows where his wire cutters are.

HOW TO BE IN TIME MORE OFTEN

TIP #1 - STRATEGICALLY WAIT UNTIL THE LAST MINUTE

Some moments require urgency, but not everything you are asked to do will be urgent. Instead, consider how you can learn the art of *strategic procrastination*. Here's a perfect example from daily life: If you run out of milk at home, do you immediately go to the store to get more or do you add it to some type of shopping list to pick up later (usually along with other things)?

This is a form of strategic procrastination—you are waiting to do something until you can optimize your time doing it. Consider treating the things you are asked to do at work with this same mentality. Spend an hour sending email, then close your email and don't look at it again for several hours at least. Productive people are intentional about how they spend their time ... and about what they choose to procrastinate and do later.

TIP #2 - Be in the Moment

There are many ways to distract yourself today thanks to information overload, social networks, and the temptation to stay connected in every moment. To improve my own ability to stay in the moment, last year I spent a month trying various things to remove all technological interruptions from my day. I turned off *every* alert on my mobile phone. I removed most social networks from the home screen of my phone and instead created a folder system that required me, for example, to click three times in order to even get to Instagram. I removed all games from my phone. And I made a mental commitment to never use my phone during a meal and started keeping it in my bag instead of my pocket so it was less accessible (and therefore less tempting to quickly check).

You don't have to be quite as extreme, but the discipline of setting rules for yourself around technology use is critical to training yourself to be in the moment instead of spending *every* moment buried in your phone.

TIP #3 - Do More "Just-in-Time" Learning

Just-in-time education doesn't need to be as formal as a training course. It can happen every time you prepare for a meeting or learn a new skill in anticipation for a new day. When I decided to start my own publishing company, I had to give myself a crash course in everything from the intricacies of choosing various types of lamination and spot UV gloss coatings for book printing to how BISAC codes and publishing metadata worked.

To do it, I hired freelance publishing experts and paid them hourly to answer every question I could come up with. I read publications, attended training courses, and surrounded myself with real experts in everything from how printing presses work to indexing. Over the next two years, I probably earned the equivalent of a master's degree in publishing and production—all of which made my publishing company better.

PART III

COMMUNICATE BETTER

CHAPTER 10

MAKE OTHERS CRY

THE SECRET: TELL BETTER STORIES

WHEN SELF-MADE HOLLYWOOD AGENT AND MOVIE PRODUCER Jerry Weintraub decided to remake the old Frank Sinatra film *Ocean's Eleven,* he had the crazy idea to get nearly a dozen of the hottest actors in Hollywood at the time to be part of the film. Everyone in the industry told him the idea was impossible because it would require each of them to take a huge pay cut. Weintraub decided to try anyway. His first step was to visit two friends he knew and respected: actor George Clooney and director Steven Soderbergh. He managed to convince them both to be part of the film and lead the charge to recruit the other actors.

Despite this early victory, it was obvious that no film (even one with a big budget) could afford to pay millions of dollars each to a dozen actors all used to being cast in a leading role. As Weintraub recalls in his personal memoir, *When I Stop Talking, You'll Know I'm Dead*, getting the rest of the actors was all thanks to the relationships and storytelling abilities of Clooney and Soderbergh.

The two personally went to each star and used creative storytelling to convince them to be part of the ensemble cast for a fraction of what they would usually make per film. For example, when they sent the script to Julia Roberts (who at the time was getting $20 million per movie), they attached a twenty-dollar bill along with a note that said, "We know you get twenty for a movie, but you will have to work for a little less on this one." Once she agreed to do it, they used a similar approach to sign Andy Garcia, Matt Damon, Don Cheadle, and Brad Pitt—all of who said yes because so many of their peers had also joined the project.

The story behind the making of *Ocean's Eleven* is a powerful reminder of the impact of relationships and stories. When you make your pitch emotional and use a story, people remember it and you get a response. Sometimes the right story might even inspire a tear or two—and make people cry.

It is easy to understand why an actor and director would tell a story in order to convince fellow actors to join a project, but how well does this work outside of an industry built for storytellers? As some of the latest scientific research into the neuroscience of how humans process information proves, stories work better than almost anything else because our brains are hard-wired to use emotion as a critical factor in making decisions.

STORIES ARE EMOTIONAL

Over the past decade, a host of best-selling books from *Sway* to *Predictably Irrational* all share the central premise that emotions are far more important than logic when it comes to our decision-making. In his groundbreaking book, *The Political Brain,* noted psychologist Drew Westen showed that emotions even inform who we choose to vote for. The point of all this research is to expose the myth that decisions are best made logically by weighing pros and cons.

. . . .

The fact that we all rely on our emotions to make decisions is not a bad thing. It is a human thing.

. . . .

While it is sometimes underappreciated in a business world that seems to run on PowerPoint and bullet points, the most admired speakers and leaders in the world, from Nelson Mandela to Bill Clinton, are routinely the ones who understand this truth. Famed film studios like Pixar or advertisers like Coca-Cola all understand this as well.

In films or books or advertising, stories have the ability to bring ideas to life. They create understanding. And when used in the right moment, they can help you to make a lot of money as well.

THE $26-MILLION NECKLACE

Lynda Resnick may be one of the most brilliant entrepreneurs and marketers of the past twenty years that most people have never heard of. Though she may not be a household name like Elon Musk or Richard Branson, the brands she has been at the heart of creating are far more recognizable.

The company she owns along with her husband, Stewart, is behind the creation and marketing of Fiji water, POM Wonderful juice, and Wonderful Pistachios. She branded mandarin oranges as "Cuties" and then later as "Halos." The best example of her storytelling intuition, however, comes from a legendary moment when she bought a string of imitation pearls from the estate of Jacqueline Kennedy Onassis from a Sotheby's auction.

Those pearls were already a part of American history thanks to the many photos immortalizing them as the favorite jewelry of choice for "Jackie O"— as the former First Lady and wife of assassinated U.S. President John F. Kennedy was affectionately known by the American public. The bidding for her pearl necklace was expected to start at around $25,000, and Resnick ultimately bought it for a whopping $211,000.

Despite what you may be thinking, this was not a randomly extravagant indulgence from an eccentric billionaire. After completing her purchase, Resnick immediately commissioned an exact replica to be made, packaged it along with a beautiful notecard and images of Jackie O. wearing the necklace and partnered with a television shopping channel to quickly sell more than 130,000 of these replicas at $200 each ... for a net profit of more than $26 million. What made the necklace so appealing?

After buying it, women felt connected to an iconic part of American history. When they wore the necklace, they had a powerful story to share with the people they met. As Resnick told former Sony Pictures CEO and author Peter Guber, who recounted this example in his book *Tell To Win*, the story was the key, and the value of telling it well was a net profit of millions of dollars.

WHY PEOPLE FOLLOW STORIES

Reading this example, it might seem a little too easy. Can you really just tell a good story and expect it to sell for millions of dollars? One of the most interesting truths about people is that the higher up you go, the more likely they are to trust their intuition about you.

My second book, *Likeonomics,* focused on the reasons why we so often buy from and do business with people that we like. Personal connections are much more easily forged through storytelling—and trust can be built the same way.

. . . .

Before anyone will believe you, they have to believe *in* you.

. . . .

You may not always have a meeting with the CEO or even a key decision maker. To understand the power of storytelling, you don't need to grace the inside of a boardroom. Just look at one of the most common behaviors in social media and you'll see this principle in action every day.

What is the #1 item shared on social media consistently? Stories—from the news media or elsewhere. Beyoncé's pregnancy picture was the most liked Instagram photo of all time. Why? Because it shows an engaging human side of the pop star in a powerful yet vulnerable way.

This highlights one of the most important things the social psychologists who study the transmission of ideas find over and over again: people respond to and share *stories* far more often than they share *facts*.

It is also why I currently teach storytelling along with marketing at Georgetown and why so many companies are hungry to train their teams on how to be better storytellers.

HOW TO TELL BETTER STORIES

TIP #1 - SHOW DON'T TELL

If I told you that Costco founder James Sinegal—whose warehouse store has one of the lowest employee turnover rates in retail—believes in a flat style of management, that would be true but unremarkable. Instead, what if I told you the true story about how every day when Sinegal went into stores around the country, he never traveled without his standard Costco nametag (which simply says "JIM") and always greeted employees by their first name while making a point of asking about their families.[9] This is clearly a "flat" style of management, but the story makes it more personal and memorable and tells you far more about him as a leader. It is even more powerful because it is not even him who needs to tell the story. Employees do that for him because his actions send such a powerful message.

TIP #2 - Make It Personal

Stories need real characters, and one of the biggest mistakes that people often make is wringing out all traces of humanity from their presentations or written work. Do you describe yourself in the third person in online profiles or in the first person? One of the most basic ways to bring the human element of storytelling back is to switch back to the first person and to make sure that the stories you are sharing include real people and situations. As you can see with this book, I'm sharing many of my own personal stories and stories of others as a way to give you some insight into my life as well as other memorable examples to learn from. My hope is that making it personal will help the ideas I share in the book to stay in your mind for longer.

TIP #3 - Take Inspiration from History

When I deliver a keynote talk about the power of storytelling to build trust, one story I share to offer context around the power (and ethics) of storytelling is the historical tale of how cinnamon was once sold. This spice has a surprisingly interesting backstory, which at one time involved Middle Eastern spice traders inventing the furious "cinnamologus" bird that (according to myth) built its nests on clifftops out of cinnamon sticks. According to the story, since the only way to harvest cinnamon was for hunters to heroically climb these cliffs and battle the bird to steal the sticks, the high price of cinnamon at the time seemed justifiable.[10]

Sadly for the traders, it was only a matter of time before their hoax was revealed. My point in sharing this on stage is to remind my audience that stories can be used in positive ways or as a tool for manipulation, so it is up to them to think and act ethically. Using the historical tale of cinnamon makes this point much more powerful and memorable than it would be otherwise.

CHAPTER 11

Interrupt Often

THE SECRET: BE AN ACTIVE LISTENER

In a recent poll among daytime TV watchers of their favorite talk show host of all time, the overwhelming choice for the top spot was Ellen DeGeneres.[11] You don't need the poll results to see how Ellen's reputation at conducting candid and powerful interviews precedes her. It has made her a natural choice to interview some of the biggest celebrities in the world.

Routinely over her career, she interviewed everyone from movie stars to music icons to world leaders. Part of the reason is the size and loyalty of her audience and how much trust she has built with them, but the real reason she is considered such an elite interviewer has very little to do with the one thing you might assume she is great at: listening.

THE TRUTH ABOUT ELLEN'S LISTENING SKILLS

It is easy to credit Ellen's ability to be a good listener as the reason why she does such great interviews. No one could do the types of interviews she does *without* being a great listener. Most of us spend plenty of years growing up learning just how important it is to be a good listener. Since preschool, we learn that we have two ears and one mouth for a reason. Or if that cliché doesn't resonate for you, I'm sure I could come up with about a dozen others about the importance of listening.

The problem is, most of the time we aren't really taught *what* good listening really means. Instead, we learn how to *silently* listen … which usually means shutting up and trying to pay attention to someone else.

What if listening (or silent listening) isn't the best way to have a powerful conversation or conduct an interview? What if the real key to being a good listener is learning to be a strategic *interrupter*?

THE ART OF INTERRUPTION

If you re-watch any interview Ellen has ever done, you'll notice an interesting balance that she manages to strike between listening and interrupting. In some moments, she will listen intently and ask leading questions. But then as the conversation starts, she will reflect on something that her guest says. She might interject with a story of her own. And she will interrupt often.

Instead of doing it in a self-serving or mean way, though, she does it with a rhythm that allows her conversations to continue and get deeper. Her interruptions help the conversation flow and uncover more interesting insights. Learning the art of interruption could do the same for your conversations with anyone if you could master how to do it. Though it may seem counterintuitive, when done right interruptions can create *more* interaction. This is what it means to be an active listener instead of a passive one.

HOW TO BE AN ACTIVE LISTENER

TIP #1 - NOD LESS, ASK FOR DETAIL

Executive coach Olivia Fox Cabane teaches leaders how to have more charisma. In her process, which she writes about in her book *The Charisma Myth*, one of the first techniques she teaches her clients is to reduce the frequency with which they nod when listening. Her tip of learning to control your natural impulse to nod too often helps reduce the perception that you're just impatiently waiting until it is your chance to speak. If someone shares, for example, that they just came back from a vacation, instead of nodding as they launch into the same stories they have probably shared with many others, you might ask them if there was a moment on the trip that changed them? Or if there was one place where they wished time would stand still? These are not the same questions people usually ask, and so they can be great ways to offer a *strategic* interruption that creates a deeper conversation than you might otherwise have.

TIP #2 - Use Reflecting Phrases

One of the techniques that trained counselors are taught is employing the use of reflecting phrases to mirror what someone is saying. For example, "what I heard you say was…" or "the thing I found interesting about that was…" This type of reflection is something Ellen does frequently as well, often repeating key phrases that interviewees say to reinforce a point that viewers might have missed. No matter what kind of phrase you prefer, the idea is to get better at using these so you can have them in your conversational toolkit to help you be a more active listener.

TIP #3 - Follow the Scene

In improvisational acting, you never want to "close" a scene by inadvertently creating a dead end. The rule in improv is that you accept the premise. For example, if the act starts and someone asks you what it was like growing up on a farm, you never protest by saying, "But I grew up in the city!" If you do, the scene is dead. Instead, you have to go with the premise. In improv, they call this a "yes and" mindset.[12]

So in the above scene, you might start talking about what it was like to take care of animals or how you did grow up there but what you really wanted was to be something else. Conversations work much the same way as this improvised scene. When you can use open-ended questions to inspire someone to share a story with you and add to the topic, your conversation will become deeper and more meaningful as a result.

CHAPTER 12

NEVER EAT CAULIFLOWER

THE SECRET: HAVE A POINT OF VIEW

I ACTIVELY HATE CAULIFLOWER.

It is and has always been my least favorite "food." I hate the smell, the look, and the texture of it. I think it barely deserves to be called food. There was a time when I used to keep my disdain for cauliflower to myself. I'd smile politely and quietly avoid it. I might have even taken some on my plate to please a particularly overbearing host ... especially since cauliflower is a very common ingredient in a lot of Indian dishes—and it is almost impossible to refuse food from an Indian host!

Then one day I decided I would stop pretending. From that day onward, if I was invited to dinner and someone asked if there was anything I didn't eat, I had my answer ready. I would single out cauliflower.

Some people would smile. Some would ask if I was allergic (I'm not). The most ambitious would try to convince me that I would almost certainly love it if I could just try that one magical recipe which only they know about. I always refuse with a smile.

. . . .

There is nothing anyone can do to cauliflower to make it something humans should eat.

. . . .

Now before you dismiss me as a picky eater, I should tell you that I am quite the opposite.

I've tried deep-fried crickets on the streets of Hong Kong. I had whale tartare in Norway. On a recent trip to China, I was the only one in our group (Chinese included) who was excited to order and taste sautéed pig's kidneys. If you told me something was a delicacy in a strange land, I would probably take a bite just to know what it tastes like. I am the sort of traveler who always tries everything.

Except for cauliflower.

Over time, though, something interesting started to happen when it came to my dislike of cauliflower. My unapologetic public hatred for it became a way for people to get to know something unexpectedly personal about me. Just as newly dating couples eventually figure out how their partner likes their coffee, my "cauliphobia" as I sometimes jokingly called it, was a small quirky fact about me that people remembered.

Yes, it sounds strange. But I started bonding with people over my intense dislike of a vegetable—and my willingness to share it.

SOME PEOPLE BELIEVE...

One of the most basic skills that many lawyers learn early in their law school training is how to make a qualified statement without revealing a personal bias.

In order to project what is often called "confident uncertainty," they will use words like *appears, seems, suggests,* or *indicates*. They will start sentences with "some people believe..." or similar lead-ins.

It works in the legal environment, where opinions can and may be held against you in a court of law. In the business world and real life, though, having opinions is highly desirable.

· ·

Having an opinion usually makes the difference between whether you are adding value to a situation or just mindlessly following orders.

· ·

We seek out people who have a point of view. We listen to advice from them. We look for them to lead us. Yet this is not an open invitation to be closed minded either. You don't have to say something that everyone around you agrees with. You do, however, have to be able to argue *for* what you believe—even if it happens to be as silly as hating cauliflower.

People with a point of view aren't pushovers. They earn respect because of the strength of their own convictions, but they are also willing to evolve the way they think.

BE PERSUADABLE

Decades ago, when asked about the rise in anti-intellectualism that was happening in the world, science fiction writer Isaac Asimov famously pointed out that "there is a cult of ignorance in the United States... nurtured by the false notion that democracy means that 'my ignorance is just as good as your knowledge'."

Having a point of view is great—but not when it is based on ignorance. My hatred of cauliflower may be illogical, but it is not uninformed. I am tragically well informed about the disgusting flavor of that vegetable and even used to eat it as a child.

In matters of taste, you can always have your opinion. When it comes to bigger things, it is important to learn how to be what author Al Pittampalli calls "persuadable" in his book of the same title.

. . . .

Being persuadable means being willing to update your beliefs when confronted with evidence that they may be wrong.

. . . .

It also means taking the perspective of others (something we learned about in Chapter 8).

This is the balance that is hard but necessary to strike—between having enough strength to build your own point of view and defend it, while also remaining open minded enough to evolve your beliefs when presented with new information or facts.

HOW TO HAVE A POINT OF VIEW

TIP #1 - LEARN TO SEPARATE BELIEF FROM FACT

. . . .

It has always been difficult for any one of us to separate the things that we believe from the things that could objectively be proven as facts. The media we consume can be biased in either direction, and it can lead to mistaken assumptions and the ability for anyone to prove any point simply by twisting "facts" into one direction or another. When you add this to the epidemic of fake news online, it is a perfect storm for masking the truth.

Yet the upside of this 24/7 media environment is that you always have the means to access verifiable facts if you are deliberate about crafting a point of view from a variety of sources. In fact, this skill of navigating media bias is so important that a host of high schools and universities across the world are now teaching "news literacy" as a basic skill each of us will need in order to succeed in the world.

TIP #2 - DON'T BE A DUMBASS

If there is one promise that many liberal arts colleges make, it is to teach their students how to think. Learning how to think, though, doesn't require a college degree (though the discipline that it takes to earn one can be valuable in itself). It does require you to have enough confidence to form your own point of view and ask questions to inform it whenever you can.

> Being a dumbass means choosing to believe what you want despite the absence of any facts, evidence or ability to argue for it.

If I complained about the flavor of cauliflower and hated it without ever having tried it ... that would make me a dumbass. Choosing to be uninformed or arguing for something simply because you believe it without any sort of evidence or experience is just plain stupid. You can and should choose to be better than that.

TIP #3 - TAKE AN UNPOPULAR POSITION

One of the hallmarks of a "yes-man" or "yes-woman" is agreeing with everything the boss says blindly. Yet psychologists who study human behavior know that agreeing with others in a large group is a natural thing to do. Psychologists call this the "spiral of silence," where members of a group become fearful of isolation and gravitate to share the opinion of the vocal majority.

The best way to combat this effect is a technique often used in debate classes ... occasionally take an unpopular position *deliberately* so you can challenge yourself to argue for it. This little action, though sometimes infuriating to the people around you, can do wonders for your ability to craft your own more powerful point of view because you have been forced to consider an opposing point of view and see the world through the eyes of someone who believes something different than you.

CHAPTER 13

WRITE ON WALLS WITH A SHARPIE

THE SECRET: SIMPLIFY EVERYTHING

JUST OVER A DECADE AGO, A PRINCETON UNIVERSITY RESEARCHER named Daniel M. Oppenheimer conducted a fascinating experiment that should be required reading for any college professor handing out writing assignments to students.[13]

In the experiment, undergraduate students were asked anonymously to share how often they would use larger words in writing assignments to appear more intelligent. Not surprisingly, a majority admitted to doing this often. Oppenheimer then analyzed how people who *read* those same assignments were likely to describe the intelligence of the person writing them.

You might expect that those students using big words and complex descriptions might have been perceived as more intelligent. Instead, Oppenheimer uncovered the opposite seemed to be true.

. . . .

In other words, *the more unnecessarily sophisticated words you used, the dumber people thought you were.*

. . . .

Simplicity rather than complexity was the secret, but it can be extremely hard to do well. And it takes more time too. There is a reason why most government and legal documents are long and complex. Making them shorter and more meaningful would require real work and more time—which is often in short supply.

Yet taking more time alone won't necessarily help you to simplify your ideas either. What if there was a technique that any of us could use to simplify just about any idea, without losing its essence?

SHARPIES AND POST-ITS

There is a fellow named Dan Roam who has spent a good part of his professional life developing a technique to answer this very question. His best-selling book, *Back of the Napkin,* offers the idea that the toughest challenges you will face in your professional career or personal life can usually be simplified (and overcome) if you just learn how to draw them.

He travels around the world teaching workshops on the topic of how to solve problems with pictures and has trained thousands of professionals on how to go from an "I can't draw" mentality, to picking up a Sharpie and starting to sketch.

One of his biggest lessons, though, is one that I uncovered by accident years before reading his book while I was working on a storyboard for a crucial pitch. At the time, I was part of a global sales team working to win multi-million dollar advertising contracts from major brands and our method for preparing our presentations involved building out the "story" of our pitch in visual form—very similar to how filmmakers block out their film storylines.

In this particular case, I was trying desperately to simplify our argument and decided to write a sequence of arguments on some small Post-it notes. The only pen I had close by was a Sharpie brand marker. As I started using it, I quickly realized that the combination of a thick Sharpie and limited space on a Post-it note meant I could only fit a few words on each note.

Suddenly the way I described vague ideas mattered. I had to pick the right words because I had no room for rambling. It forced me to simplify.

THE SIMPLICITY ADVANTAGE

The power of simplicity, it turns out, isn't just limited to how you might describe words or ideas—or what pen you use to describe them (even though I'm partial to Sharpies!). Some of the most successful products and companies of our modern era owe a large part of their success to an unwavering focus on simplicity.

In his biography of Steve Jobs, writer Walter Isaacson credited Apple's unwavering focus on simplicity as the force that helped it become, at one time, the most valuable company in the world. In more recent years since Steve Jobs passed away, other brands have taken the lead on this idea.

Snapchat. Amazon. Warby Parker. Netflix. Each is a brand or product that has simplicity built into the experience they offer to their customers. These brands stand out for being simpler than their competitors. And in an increasingly complex world, that may turn out to be the ultimate competitive advantage for brands and people alike.

HOW TO SIMPLIFY EVERYTHING

TIP #1 - BEWARE THE CURSE OF KNOWLEDGE

Before wrapping my dust jacket over their book, one of the things I learned from *Made to Stick* authors Chip and Dan Heath was about "the curse of knowledge." Here's how they explain it: "The problem is that once we know something—say, the melody of a song—we find it hard to imagine not knowing it. Our knowledge has 'cursed' us. We have difficulty sharing it with others because we can't readily re-create their state of mind. We start to forget what it is like to *not* know what we know."

We all suffer from this curse at one point or another. While you can't remove your knowledge, you *can* start to overcome it by becoming more conscious of the things that you might take for granted. One great way to do that is to force yourself to explain what you know to more people unfamiliar with that topic. The more you practice and see what people "get" and what they don't, the more you can grow your ability to simplify.

TIP #2 – DRAW INSTEAD OF TALK

Many people learn better from visuals than they do from words. This means that drawing may not only help you to visualize a solution to a complex problem, it may also be the *only* way to explain it to a large group of people. In one often retold example, a pilot and a lawyer were having a drink in a San Antonio bar back in 1966. On a cocktail napkin, the pair drew a triangle to symbolize the business plan for a new airline they aimed to start. It would fly several times a day, seven days a week between the three points of the triangle, which represented Texas cities Houston, Dallas, and San Antonio.

That conversation led to the founding of Southwest Airlines, and that legendary cocktail napkin is today commemorated on a plaque at the airline's headquarters.[14]

TIP #3 - USE PLAIN LANGUAGE

In school, your English class may have emphasized something that doesn't necessarily lead to success in the workplace: the use of big words to showcase your vocabulary. Showing off your prodigiously erudite vocabulary is useful for high school English papers, winning in Scrabble and surviving graduate comparative literature courses. I should know ... I did a master's degree in English literature. When it comes to interactions in the workplace, though, your vocabulary doesn't need to be chock-full of fourteen-letter whoppers. Instead, try to write the way that you would speak out loud. Checking to see if you're doing this right is easy—just print out any piece of writing and read it out loud to yourself. If it doesn't sound like something you would say, change it.

PART IV

CONNECT BETTER

CHAPTER 14

LEAVE YOUR TOYS OUT

THE SECRET: BE A CONNECTOR

My house is filled with Legos.

Unfortunately, they are not contained neatly in a box or in a playroom. Our Legos have a habit of spreading out. They hide inside of couches. They create painful landmines for unsuspecting bare feet to step on early in the morning. But despite their ability to travel to inconvenient places, I love Legos.

As a father of two boys, I have spent hours building towers and spaceships with them. When we first started, the easiest thing to build was a tower. All you had to do was stack one Lego piece on top of another, going as high as you could until the whole thing would collapse from its own instability.

There is a trick, though, that can stabilize just about anything you make with Legos: you need to overlap them.

When you do that, you can build a foundation that won't break apart. You get stability. At some point, this is the secret every kid needs to learn before building a stronger spaceship or a taller tower.

After you use this trick, you don't break down your creation immediately. You add to it and enjoy it because it took more effort to make. You end up doing the one thing your parents probably told you not to do ... you leave your toys out.

What if you did the same thing with relationships? It is easy to focus on making as many connections as possible. This business-card-collecting mentality is the same as trying to build that Lego tower as tall as possible. It seems impressive, but it's one move away from collapsing.

Instead, the best relationships overlap.

. . . .

Rather than *collecting* relationships via business cards or online friend requests, the most successful people focus on *introducing* their connections to one another.

. . . .

They overlap their relationships and become connectors. That is even more important when you consider the growing body of evidence that there may be a limit to how many truly valuable social connections you can actually have.

WHY SCIENCE SAYS YOU CAN ONLY HAVE 150 FRIENDS

After two decades of research on the nature of social connections, an anthropologist named Robin Dunbar came across the curious story of an entrepreneur named Bill Gore, inventor of the now famous GORE-TEX material. At one point after walking his factory floors, Gore realized that the more people his factory hired, the less likely his employees were to work hard or feel connected to a community. To combat this growing disconnection, he took a bold step that surprised most of his employees ... and his investors.

Gore decided to limit each one of his factories to 150 workers. As the company grew, he would just build a new factory and install a similar cap on employees at each factory. Morale and sense of community soared. The result was pronounced, but it was the number that interested Dunbar most. It echoed his own research which had proposed that 150 was the approximate number of individuals that any one person could maintain stable relationships with at any given moment.

The science behind Dunbar's Number[15] (as it is now called), suggests that we can only build real and authentic relationships with a limited number of people. In an age filled with thousands of social media connections, this number may seem hard to believe. Chances are you already have ten times that many connections across the various social platforms you use.

Yet despite all these surface connections, the truth is there is a natural human limit to the number of people we can truly get to know—and over time the people that make up that inner circle of friendship is bound to change.

At the same time, you already know that the people who tend to have the most success in life are the ones who manage to surround themselves with the right people and build their network as a powerful asset for their careers and personal lives.

NEVER EAT ALONE

What does it take to build this type of network for yourself? More importantly, how can you make the right moves to grow your network *before* you are in a moment when you desperately need it to find a new job or to start over in a new city without the safety net of friends or family?

According to Keith Ferrazzi, author of *Never Eat Alone: And Other Secrets to Success, One Relationship at a Time*, one of the keys to doing this well is to join conversations before you start them and to stop keeping score.

The underlying message of his advice is clear ... be unselfish, think about how to help others before helping yourself, and be generous with your time and connections.

These are the foundation of building a powerful network.

HOW TO BE A CONNECTOR

TIP #1 - Solve Problems with Introductions

At any given moment, anyone you meet will probably be struggling with *something* they could use help with at work or in life, but may not feel comfortable bringing up directly in conversation. It may be that they need a new member of their team. Or they are trying to coordinate a cross country move with their family. Or they want to eat healthier. We all have daily struggles that we grapple with, both professionally and personally.

> One of the best ways to make powerful connections is to see yourself as a problem solver.

This is not, however, an invitation to give unsolicited (and usually unwanted) advice. Instead, the "solution" you should think about offering is an introduction to someone else who might be able to offer more direct help.

If you can be the connector to put someone who needs help together with another person who can offer it, both people will usually remember the favor. Though you shouldn't expect it, some will even find a way to repay that favor in the future.

TIP #2 – Go Beyond Swiping Right

It is easy to swipe right or left on a photo in a dating app. It is harder to think like a professional matchmaker. If you think about that job, matchmakers spend time getting to know the people they work with. They understand their motivations and their philosophy of the world. Their aim is always to learn enough about someone to find another person who may be compatible. They are experts at seeing similarities instead of differences. Though you are probably not getting paid to do this as matchmakers usually are, doing the same thing when *you* see similarities either through interest or job roles or geography or any other reason involves being proactive and following up. You don't need to wait for someone to ask. If a connection makes sense, be the person who takes the initiative to make it happen.

TIP #3 – Get Out of the Way

Sometimes the best connections require only an introduction and nothing more. Knowing when to get out of the way and let great conversations happen without you is extremely hard to learn. It can feel like you're being left out, but connections take on their own life and the truth is that you need to be prepared for some of them to happen without you.

Rather than letting the FOMO (Fear Of Missing Out) part of your brain let you start to worry about what you're missing out on, think about making connections the same way most of us think about recommending a restaurant. Just because you suggest a place to eat doesn't mean you expect to be invited along every time someone goes there.

Relationships and connections sometimes need the same type of space. It is okay when your friends become friends. Sometimes they will get closer to one another than they are to you. Remind yourself that this has probably happened in your case, too.

CHAPTER 15

Rip Your Jeans

THE SECRET: INVITE MORE SERENDIPITY

In many industries, it is a long-standing belief that there are two kinds of people: suits and creatives. The "suits" handle the money and manage the accounts. The "creatives" wear jeans (or whatever they want), come up with the big ideas and deliver on them.

It is no coincidence workers are described by what they wear. Over my career, I have worked at some of the biggest advertising agencies in the world launching marketing campaigns for brands like Intel, Kellogg's, Ford, IBM and many others.

Across multiple roles in multiple countries, I had the unique chance to alternate between roles: for some clients,

I was the suit; for others, I was the creative. Almost every day I saw proof that what you wear describes your role in a powerful way to the people around you. Yet this lesson was about more than just "dressing for success" or wearing a suit to an interview. Anyone can tell you to do that.

When I first moved from Australia back to the U.S. after working in advertising for five years, my idea of dressing for success meant wearing ripped jeans and a designer shirt. For a pitch, I might wear a sports coat.

For the team managing the conservative Washington, D.C. office of the large agency where I'd started working in 2004, though, the dress code was unofficially a suit and usually a tie. In that office, creatives and suits *both* wore suits.

I wore jeans anyway.

At least I did right up until I had "the talk" with HR, which concluded with a promise that if I wore jeans to work one more time (and especially ones with holes in them), I would promptly be fired.

THAT TIME WHEN I STOPPED WEARING JEANS ...

Naturally, I stopped wearing jeans. I needed the job.

I retreated into my office, shut the door (yes, it was the first and last time that I ever had an actual office with a door!), and focused on my work. I delivered on the projects I needed to deliver. I called the meetings I needed to call.

But in addition to losing my jeans, I lost something intangible that I'd had in my previous roles: some of my creative energy.

A few months after HR delivered its ultimatum, I started working on a project that involved traveling every week to work with colleagues in the New York office. In New York, people wore what they wanted. They created freely and their office was designed to encourage and inspire. More important, creative people seemed happier in their roles. They tended to stay in their roles longer than their D.C.-based counterparts.

When I went to New York, I usually wore jeans. My clothes reflected my day, but I started to realize that they were also helping me open myself up to another equally important element of success: serendipity.

As I became more comfortable, I felt freer to think differently. I didn't feel the need to schedule meetings for every interaction. I could be inspired by conversations. But couldn't all of this have happened if I had worn a suit too? For me, in that environment, the clear answer was no.

Wearing jeans helped me make unexpected connections. It helped me to more easily be myself and remember to leave that office door open to welcome new conversations.

Of course, as an advertising guy working on creative ideas all day, jeans were my "uniform." That doesn't have to be the case for everyone. Your version of jeans could be anything. It may even be a doctor's coat.

THE WHITE COAT EFFECT

A few years ago, a team of researchers at Northwestern University published a study in the *Journal of Experimental Social Psychology* where they found that students who believed they were wearing a doctor's coat exhibited a heightened sense of attention than those who believed they were not. Both groups had on the same coat.[16]

This so-called White Coat Effect is easy to believe when you imagine the days in your own life when you feel more or less confident based on the clothes that you have chosen to wear. The interesting side effect of this clothing-induced self-confidence is that it has an impact on how other people see you and choose to interact with you as well.

HOW TO INVITE MORE SERENDIPITY

TIP #1 – DRESS FOR THE SITUATION, NOT THE CODE

Is success really about wearing jeans on Wall Street? Not so much. If you do that it would be hard to be taken seriously in that environment. The way you dress has to send the right message in the environment you are in. No matter how much I may have disliked wearing a suit and tie or felt it didn't fit my personality, if I had a big pitch meeting with a governmental organization or a top-tier bank, I usually went with the suit and tie. Not only was it a standard requirement of the situation, but also my audience was likely to see it as a sign of disrespect if I did not. For everyday work and life, the most important thing is to focus on the situation.

TIP #2 - Find a Way to Share Your Personality

One of my big mistakes when following the no-jeans mandate was letting that affect the way I would express myself. No matter what situation you happen to be in, or what dress code you need to adhere to, there is usually still an opportunity to express your personality.

Maybe you have trendy "statement" glasses or sport cowboy boots or wear quirky mismatched dress socks. Whatever your choice, finding a way to be yourself (even in a work culture that discourages it) can do wonders for your ability to remain open to unexpected serendipitous opportunities instead of letting them pass you by.

TIP #3 – SHOW YOUR APPROACHABILITY

Serendipity comes from being open to having conversations with new people, but it also comes from showing your approachability in a way that people don't expect. For example, when I am at an event in a group conversation and there is someone else nearby with no one to speak to—I always invite them to join our group. I make sure I'm not accidentally standing with my back facing toward someone. You might be thinking these are extremely trivial things. Am I really telling you how to stand at a networking event?

I never focused on these things either. But once I started doing them and inviting people into conversations, I realized that a good friendly group conversation attracts more people. Being the person in the midst of that type of conversation allowed each new person who joined to feel more at ease and less like they needed to make some kind of small talk. That is the power of focusing on being approachable.

CHAPTER 16

Help People Steal

THE SECRET: SHARE THE CREDIT

AT THE END OF 2006, A LIST OF THE MOST POPULAR BLOG POSTS of the entire year (ranked by the number of other sites linking to them) was published by a popular blog directory called Technorati. Almost every one of the top 100 articles mentioned either politics or technology except for a small handful of business posts distributed between all the geeks and wonks that had made the cut.

It was a list that I had been watching closely since I had first started blogging just two years earlier. By August 2006, I was getting about twenty-five visitors a day but had aspirations to grow my audience as much as I could.

Then overnight everything changed.

On August 10, 2006, I published a blog post titled "The 5 Rules of Social Media Optimization (SMO)." In it, I described what I thought might become a new digital marketing technique that could eventually become a companion to the already exploding practice of Search Engine Optimization (SEO). Within hours, several other respected marketing bloggers shared the post and even added their own suggestions to the original post via comments. Soon my original five rules had gone up to seventeen.[17]

DON'T "OWN" THE IDEA

Over the course of the following week, dozens more people commented on the post. Random bloggers started translating the post into other languages and sharing it with their global audience in other countries. The quantifiable effect of all this attention was apparent in my website analytics: my average daily blog visitors had shot up to several thousand every day. It was fair to say that my short post about SMO had officially gone viral.

The conversation was happening at a speed that only the online environment can really enable. More people were talking about and linking to the article. It was generating dozens of new mentions online every day, and Google was steadily rewarding all that buzz by delivering more clicks to my post via search engine queries. There was even a robust (and growing) entry for the term on Wikipedia—the ultimate geek symbol that the idea had "made it."

All the attention meant that I had a choice to make.

Should I claim the idea as my own, become the "SMO guy", and pivot my entire blog to focus exclusively on SMO? Should I get a lawyer and trademark the term? That was the way to really *own* the idea, and I had been blogging long enough to know it. The only problem was that I had too many other things I enjoyed writing and talking about and couldn't imagine just focusing on this one single idea.

So I chose to do the exact opposite.

I republished the rules others had suggested as addendums to my original post. I invited others to take the rules, remix them, and share them again. I asked anyone interested in the idea to write about it freely. Within a matter of months, the original post was cited so often it did indeed become one of the few business posts to make the list of top 100 posts that year.

In the time since, thousands of people a month continued visiting my blog to read the post about SMO, and many stayed and subscribed to read my other ideas. Thanks to all the traffic and visibility, my blog was selected the following year by *AdAge* magazine as one of the top twenty-five marketing blogs in the world and the *Wall Street Journal* even featured it.

Two years later, thanks in part to the popularity of the blog and my steadily growing audience, I successfully landed a deal with McGraw-Hill, one of the largest publishers in the world, to write my first book.

BEING INTERNET FAMOUS

Beyond my one niche post about an obscure online marketing concept, this idea of a piece of content going viral online is one that we now see quite often. Writers, musicians, entertainers and all sorts of others over the past decade have the Internet to thank for growing their fan base and gaining attention. Whether you consider musicians like Ed Sheeran or personalities like comedian Lilly Singh, the path to getting discovered routinely seems to include openly sharing content and ideas and watching them spread organically instead of trying to insecurely hold onto them.

In my case, it was the combination of publishing the idea of SMO and my open choice to allow anyone to take it and use it freely that helped shape my reputation and build my audience. It helped me to stand out, build my personal brand, make amazing connections with very smart fellow marketers, and later land a five-figure book deal with a top publisher. It no longer matters whether anyone associates me with the idea of SMO or not. The idea, I'm convinced, became bigger because I didn't attempt to exert any sort of control over it. And trying to do so probably would have failed anyway.

TIP #1 - Embrace Your First Followers

In his popular TEDTalk on leadership, entrepreneur Derek Sivers shows a video of a guy doing a crazy dance on a lawn, and how it slowly starts a movement with hundreds of people recreating that same dance. In just a few minutes, he explains the often-underappreciated importance of the "first follower." The first follower "is what transforms a lone nut into a leader," he says. In order for that to happen, though, the key is that the leader must *accept* that first follower as an equal. Otherwise, the idea doesn't catch on. The lesson from his simple video and brilliant talk is clear: when it comes to letting your ideas travel, you must find your first followers, and then embrace them as co-creators of the idea.[18]

TIP #2 - Make Participation Easy

Making it easy to share and participate in your ideas is a critical part of helping to get further adoption. When TOMS shoes founder Blake Mycoskie first started his brand, the simple idea was that anyone who purchased a pair of shoes would automatically be funding a second pair to be given to someone in poverty. No extra step. No checkbox—just a charitable component that could make you feel good, baked into the process of buying a pair of TOMS no matter where you purchased them. More than a decade later, this "one-for-one" charitable business model is now something studied in MBA programs and utilized by many other retailers and charitable organizations both large and small.

TIP #3 – WELCOME REMIXING

As new people start to take your idea and share it, they will naturally want to add their own mark. Quirky.com is the perfect example of a website with a business model that intuitively understands this. If you have an idea for any type of product, you can post it on Quirky.com where the community will help to refine it. The best product ideas shared on the site are manufactured by Quirky.com into real products and then sold in retail. The power of the community comes from the fact that everyone makes a cut on the product if it gets made, from the inventor to the person who suggested the eventual product name. People are rewarded for adding their own insights to the idea and in the long run, everyone wins.

CHAPTER 17

WHY MOST GOOD ADVICE IS USELESS

IF THERE WERE A STEP-BY-STEP GUIDE ON HOW TO WRITE A BOOK about being successful, one of the requirements would probably be to have at least one chapter on the power of making mistakes. Successful people love to romanticize mistakes and the lessons they offer about life in and out of the office.

This is not a book about failing more often or even making more mistakes to fuel your learning. If anything, you could describe it as a book about *avoiding* mistakes.

WHY MISTAKES ARE OVERRATED

But wait a minute—aren't making mistakes an important part of becoming successful? Most people will tell you so. In fact, one of the places where you hear this shared most is during commencement speeches.

If you watch YouTube videos of popular commencement speeches delivered to graduating high school or college seniors every year, you'll quickly encounter four generic pieces of advice which are shared over and over again:

1. Take risks.

2. Never give up.

3. Do what you love.

4. Make mistakes.

What if there were times when each of these turned out to be extraordinarily *bad* advice?

Take risks, for example. Risks can be necessary and powerful unless they are predictably dumb wastes of money or time.

Giving up, though often underappreciated, is one of the great skills of life when you learn how to do it strategically.

. . . .

Doing what you love sounds nice, but one of the best ways to kill your passion for something is to force yourself to pay your rent immediately by doing it.

. . . .

And then we come to the advice about mistakes. At least the other three points are positive. They ask you to dream bigger.

Encouraging someone to make mistakes seems to go in the opposite direction. Why would anyone *want* to make more mistakes?

ALL MISTAKES AREN'T CREATED EQUAL

Of course, the reason successful people tell you that making mistakes is important is because they tend to remember the big ones they have made and where they led to. Yet no one gives a speech or writes a book about the seemingly stupid, microscopic mistakes we make that ruin our day or our week. Those are the ones that cause us to scratch our heads afterward and wonder how we could have been so dumb.

For example, the first time I was invited to go to Brazil to deliver a talk, I was very excited. It was one of the countries I had longed to visit for years and finally, I had my chance. The day of my flight I showed up to the airport only to realize that I had neglected to get a travel visa or even check that I needed one. The airline did not let me board, I missed my event and I looked like an idiot. Even worse, I had to forfeit my speaking fee and had disappointed my clients. *That* was dumb.

As you might imagine, the experience trained me to check multiple times on visa requirements for any new city before I travel ... but I wish I never had to learn the lesson that way. I would much rather have learned the way I did in my first real job managing web projects in Australia.

WHAT PROJECT MANAGEMENT CAN TEACH YOU ABOUT LIFE ...

As a project manager leading a team of designers and programmers to build complicated websites, I quickly learned there are two words that matters more than any others: *deadlines* and *dependencies*.

Everyone tends to focus on deadlines, but dependencies are what really control your timeline. Every task on a project usually has other tasks that must be completed first. We couldn't build a homepage, for example, until the design was done and approved. If the design was delayed, the homepage would be delayed. That's a dependency.

Now imagine that you have a project with five hundred different tasks spread out across a team of a dozen people, each with dependencies to other tasks. It gets complicated quickly. Especially if you are managing multiple projects.

I quickly learned that none of the other project managers ever created an entirely new timeline for every project. Instead, they showed me how to start with a previous project timeline—and then add or subtract tasks to customize it for your latest project.

Real life is a bit like this. We are always working to build out our own knowledge much like these templates ... with ideas and advice and life hacks. Which brings me back to the one problem left handers know well but most of the rest of us never think about.

A FINAL LESSON FROM LEFT HANDERS

When you write in English, you are writing from left to right. The problem for a leftie is that you end up smudging your writing if you use certain types of ink on certain types of paper. It is exactly the kind of small problem that only left handers know or care about.

There are many solutions lefties have developed for this frustratingly common problem. Some train themselves to write letters at a different angle to change the position of their wrist. Others slant their paper the opposite direction. One enterprising entrepreneur even invented a wearable writing glove called the "SmudgeGuard."

And then there are the left handers who skip all the fuss and just use a pencil. More than anything, this is a book about thinking like them.

Why This Book Took 4 Years to Write...

THE FIRST TIME I WROTE THIS BOOK, IT TOOK ALMOST EXACTLY three weeks. I put it online for free and over 20,000 people downloaded it.

Then I figured I should probably make *some* money on it, so I made the new price 99 cents for the ebook and another 5,000 people downloaded it. That was 2013.

Then I let it sit online for nearly four years.

When I came back to it, I realized just how much more I needed to do. The book felt unfinished. It bothered me that it wasn't as good as I knew it could be.

So I spent the past year revising, rewriting, expanding and editing. While stopping and starting, I wrote and published another book (my annual edition of *Non-Obvious*), but kept returning to this manuscript.

You hear a lot of things described as a "labor of love." Truthfully, the labor that went into rewriting this book was probably half love and half desperate necessity. It just really needed it.

The book you now hold in your hands is about 30% longer than the original with many entirely new sections. The secrets have been completely reorganized into four parts and the tips have been updated, rewritten and edited.

I share all this background to firstly explain why you might find multiple versions of this book online and also why the book says "New Updated Edition" on the cover.

It was a thrill to write this book and get it out four years ago.

It is an even bigger thrill to finally have the chance to rewrite it and say everything I wished I took the time to say the first time around.

Second chances can be a beautiful thing. I hope after reading the book, you will agree.

APPENDIX

21 Books Worth Reading

You already know that I believe life is too short to read a book that you don't find entertaining or valuable. To help you separate the best from the rest, here is my essential reading list of books that I recommend most often—curated from hundreds of possible choices.

Since this list is always evolving, you can also follow my latest reading list recommendation by visiting *www.rohitbhargava.com/bookstoread*

1. WHATEVER YOU THINK, THINK THE OPPOSITE, BY PAUL ARDEN

If there was ever a book meant to be described with the quintessentially British adjective of "cheeky," this quick read written by a legendary English advertising agency creative director Paul Arden would certainly be it. Filled with old-school creative director-isms like "Do it, then fix it as you go," this book is a nice collection of reminders to think different, be irreverent, and, above all, to intentionally design the career you want to have.

2. HOW TO WIN FRIENDS AND INFLUENCE PEOPLE, BY DALE CARNEGIE

Despite the dated writing style and references, this is one of those books that is classic for a reason. Filled with the insights Carnegie built over decades of teaching people how to present themselves, speak in public and relate to one another—the lessons you will take from this book are timeless and worth a read at any age.

3. WHAT THE CEO WANTS YOU TO KNOW, BY RAM CHARAN

As I shared in Chapter 6, the most successful employees are the ones who have the ability to see the big picture instead of being constrained by their job titles. In this book from famed CEO advisor and professor Ram Charan, you will learn the basics of business in a simple yet profound way to help you elevate your thinking far beyond your business card — no matter how many levels beneath the CEO your current job happens to be.

4. The Art of Thinking Clearly, by Rolf Dobelli (translated by Nicky Griffin)

When it was first published in German, this book quickly became a bestseller and this new translation takes the original short 99 chapters all focused on how humans make decisions and brings the easily readable stories to life for English language readers. If you happen to be someone who prefers reading books in short digestible chunks instead of long stretches, you will love the format and style of this book.

5. Mindset, by Carol Dweck

You may not realize just how much your mindset controls the success you have in life, but you will after reading this groundbreaking book, which is the product of decades of research from world-renowned Stanford psychologist Carol Dweck. Understanding the simple difference between a fixed mindset (where you believe your basic qualities like intelligence or talent are unchangeable) versus a growth mindset (where you believe anyone can be good at anything with the right amount of effort) alone is worth reading this book– and could change the way you look at life as well.

6. Pretending You Care, by Norm Feuti

A hilarious look at the sometimes-idiotic world of retail, this book by cartoonist and former retail worker Norm Feuti will be immediately familiar to anyone who has ever worked a job at the mall—and should be required reading for anyone who will work in a business where you have to inspire employees to care about what they do … or at least get better at pretending they do.

7. Tell to Win, by Peter Guber

When former Hollywood producer Peter Guber looks back on his life in this combination of a memoir and business book, it is an entertaining exploration of how the power of stories influences people. Stories include the fascinating inside account of the making of the film *Contact* with Jodie Foster to an exploration of what makes David Copperfield such an engaging performer and magician. Reading this book is like stepping behind the scenes of how movies get made, million dollar products are launched and why stories really matter.

8. Made to Stick, by Chip and Dan Heath

You might have already guessed I am a fan of this book because of my history with it, but it has a place of honor on my bookshelf for more than the size of its dust jacket. The book is well researched, engagingly written, and full of powerful lessons you will be able to put to use in your work immediately no matter what message you are trying to get to stick and who you need to believe it.

9. Steal Like an Artist, by Austin Kleon

This gem of a book is an easy read, but the counterintuitive lessons from graphic designer Austin Kleon have helped thousands of people to uncover their creative side ... even if they are not designers or people with the word "creative" in their job title. With sections on "the upside of being boring" and "what it really means to be original," the biggest benefit of this book is that it will teach you something valuable about how artists think and how you can use that in your own life, whether you describe yourself as an artist or not.

10. Einstein's Dreams, by Alan Lightman

Written as an exploration from a physicist's point of view about what Einstein's dreams might have been like if we could look inside his head, this book is nowhere near as boring as that premise might seem. At once poetic and profound, Lightman's writing will get you thinking about the nature of time and how best to spend yours. More than any other, this book changed the way I thought about life and is the one that I share most often when asked to name my favorite book.

11. Small Data, by Martin Lindstrom

You can learn something unique from a man who spends the majority of his year living in strangers' houses around the world. Consumer researcher Martin Lindstrom takes all this field research and his grueling travel schedule and uses it to share an intriguing compilation of observations about what people believe in different cultures around the world. Aside from plenty of wonderful trivia, *Small Data* also delivers a powerful exploration of the importance of really observing the world and how this one skill can help you decode why people act the way they do … and how they choose to spend their money too.

12. Disrupted, by Dan Lyons

If you have ever been romanced by the notion of the Silicon Valley inspired free-food-open-plan utopian vision of the workplace, this book offers the ethnographic wake-up call you need to read. In it, journalist Dan Lyons chronicles his time working in a rapidly growing startup as the oldest guy in the office and examines why so much of the modern workplace seems to be built on a pyramid of feel-good bullshit. A rare irreverent book that can actually make you better by showing you what dysfunction looks like and why so many people at work lose their motivation because of the inhumanity of work.

13. You Are Not So Smart, by David McRaney

This is the sort of book that is meant to be read in short chunks, with each chapter giving you a fundamental truth from years of psychology research brought to life with a modern story. Take this one with you on a short or long flight, give yourself time to think about each chapter and above all, to remind yourself that no matter how smart you think you are, there is always something you don't know.

14. To Sell Is Human, by Dan Pink

Most people recoil at the suggestion that they are acting like a sales person because it feels like an insult. We all know the stereotype of the overly pushy salesman (yes, it's usually a man). If you have ever had this sort of negative reaction to sales, this book will change your mind --- starting with the simple premise at the heart of the book: we are all in sales. Whether we are selling a product or our ideas, there are plenty of moments where we need *sell* something—but that doesn't need to make us feel sleazy or inadequate. The principles and techniques in this book will help you get better at those situations and embrace the idea of having to sell *without* becoming a pushy salesperson yourself.

15. I WILL TEACH YOU TO BE RICH, BY RAMIT SETHI

Everything that you never learned about managing your money (but should have) is in this book based on the author's popular blog of the same name. No matter how old or financially savvy you are, you will appreciate Sethi's no-nonsense approach to everything from recouping those fees your credit card charges to what types of investments are typically set up for suckers. Altogether this short and irreverent book will change how you think about managing your money, including making it, saving it, spending it, and valuing it.

16. SAVE THE CAT! BY BLAKE SNYDER

You may not believe this, but the stunning insight of this book is that *every* movie ever made uses one of just twelve different story structures. It seemed too simplistic to be true when I first read that idea in a screenwriting class, but this book from famed spec screenwriter Blake Snyder changed the way I thought about storytelling. *Save the Cat!* offers an actual formula for on-screen storytelling used by some of the best scriptwriters in the world. Though sadly, Blake passed away in 2009, his ideas are timeless and his book will change the way you think about storytelling and probably any movie you have ever watched as well.

17. The Game, by Neil Strauss

A book that exposes the slimy underworld of pickup artists and the tricks they use to lure women into bed might seem like an odd choice for this list, yet this book is much more than that. It is also a fascinating exploration of insecurity, gender dynamics, and what it really takes to be desirable (or desired). No matter your gender, you may simultaneously be intrigued and repulsed by the stories in this book, but it will teach you something important about how manipulation works. In an era filled with fake news and fake people, being able to spot when you're being hustled can keep you from getting into bed with the wrong person—figuratively _and_ literally.

Books You Should Buy (and Will Eventually Use)

In addition to the books I have recommended so far, there are some amazing resource books that I have on my shelf and recommend to everyone. You probably won't read any of them cover to cover, but they are great skimmable resources that you will most likely pick up at least once a year just to help you solve a challenge or to think in a slightly different way.

For those reasons alone, they are worth putting on your shelf until you need them. Consider this one of the few types of "just in case" education I will ever recommend.

18. WORDS THAT SELL, BY RICHARD BAYAN

Ever wanted to find the perfect word for expressing an idea and had to resort to a Google search turning up dozens of random words? You can do much better and this book will help. True to its title, the book is filled with collections of powerful sales phrases, vocabulary combinations, and words that influence and move people. Whether you're trying to write a compelling email newsletter or a powerful cover letter for your next job application, this is one of those books you'll wish you knew about earlier.

19. RESONATE, BY NANCY DUARTE

Few people have studied what makes a speech powerful as deeply as Nancy Duarte and her team. In *Resonate,* she shares the results of her extensive research into the dynamics of great talks and breaks down several world renowned speeches to share a formula for building a game-changing speech of your own. Save this book for the moment when you need to deliver an amazing talk, and then use the formula she shares to make that talk the best it can be.

20. THINKING WITH TYPE, BY ELLEN LUPTON

While this book was clearly created for visual designers, I regularly assign it for my students to refer to as a useful guidebook for what effective layout and graphic design looks like. You can't always rely on designers to do this for you—sometimes you just need to make a document look good on your own. Following the principles in this book will help you do it.

21. The Back of the Napkin, by Dan Roam

Solving your problems by drawing them is the simple idea that this book teaches (which I also shared in Chapter 13), but the step-by-step workbook-style approach and easy-to-follow instructions make this the perfect book to use as a resource when you need to uncover a solution to a complex problem. There is no better book to help you overcome that mental barrier many of us have about not being able to draw. Sometimes the *only* way to simplify something is to draw it out.

Want My Latest Reading List Recommendations?

VISIT *WWW.ROHITBHARGAVA.COM/BOOKSTOREAD*

HOW TO STAY CURIOUS

NOW THAT YOU'VE READ THE BOOK, I HAVE A FEW SUGGESTIONS for how you can keep up your sense of curiosity.

The first step is choosing to consume media and stories that are not served up by algorithms or shared by friends on social media. True curiosity involves digging past this and choosing to see more.

I spend about six hours every week reading stories and headlines from several hundred different international news sources. This ritual is part of my annual process to curate trends for my book *Non-Obvious* which is published every December ... but it is also the way that I stay informed on all kinds of topics.

Of course, I realize that most of you probably don't have as much motivation as I do to build this much time for reading and research into your usual weekly schedule.

Beyond the book, every week I also share between five and seven interesting underappreciated business stories of the week along with a short note about the significance of each and a link to the full story.

I collect these "Non-Obvious Insights" into a weekly email that goes out every Thursday morning. If this seems interesting, I would welcome you to join my list of more than ten thousand curious readers.

To sign up, just visit
WWW.ROHITBHARGAVA.COM/SUBSCRIBE

A FINAL REALITY CHECK

IS THIS BOOK SERIOUS?

You might be thinking after reading the table of contents or the cover description that some of the "secrets" shared in this book are being presented sarcastically.

When I advise you to start smoking or be a cross dresser or interrupt more often—I must be exaggerating, right?

I am not.

But if you are thinking that, I am guessing that you probably haven't read the book yet and just skipped directly to this section out of curiosity. That's ok—I would probably do the same thing.

So just to be clear: I am indeed serious about every single secret I share here and have specifically chosen the way they are presented because I want entice you to dig into the stories behind them.

Any well-meaning advice book can tell you to do what you love or have more self-confidence. None will tell you about the upside of learning to interrupt more often. Or that cross-dressing *does* improve your empathy. Or that telling better stories *will* make more people cry.

These are all good things.

So now that you know the stories and secrets in this book are serious, I hope you will go back and read it. Consider this a sort of introduction to the book, put at the end for those impatient souls who will skip to the end of a book and read that first.

I know you jumped here because I'm just like you. And if we already have that in common, my guess is you'll find much more in the book that we share as well. There's only one way to find out.

Take some time and read it.

BOOKS CITED

The 4-Hour Workweek: Escape 9-5, Live Anywhere, and Join the New Rich *by Tim Ferriss*

Deep Survival: Who Lives, Who Dies, And Why *by Laurence Gonzales*

Learned Optimism: How To Change Your Mind And Your Life *by Dr. Martin Seligman*

When I Stop Talking, You'll Know I'm Dead: Useful Stories From A Persuasive Man *by Jerry Weintraub*

Sway: The Irresistible Pull of Irrational Behavior *by Ori and Rom Brafman*

Predictably Irrational: The Hidden Forces That Shape Our Decisions *by Dan Ariely*

The Political Brain: The Role of Emotion in Deciding the Fate of the Nation *by Drew Westen*

Tell To Win: Connect, Persuade, and Triumph with the Hidden Power of Story *by Peter Guber*

The Charisma Myth: How Anyone Can Master the Art and Science of Personal Magnetism *by Olivia Fox Cabane*

Persuadable: How Great Leaders Change Their Minds to Change the World *by Al Pittampalli*

The Back Of The Napkin: Solving Problems and Selling Ideas with Pictures *by Dan Roam*

Made To Stick: Why Some Ideas Survive and Others Die *by Chip and Dan Heath*

Never Eat Alone: And Other Secrets to Success, One Relationship at a Time *by Keith Ferrazzi and Tahl Raz*

3 Reasons To Share This Book

Now that you've reached the official end of the book, I would like to offer a short pitch with three quick reasons why you should take these 15 secrets and bring them to your friends, family, workplace or school.

Reason #1: You Can Be The Connector

Books can offer a powerful credibility boost. Dumb people skim headlines. Smart people read books. The smartest people are the ones who introduce others to books and make connections. You can build your reputation as a person like that, and sharing books like this one can help.

Reason #2: You Can Elevate The Assholes

It is almost impossible to be happy in work or life if you are surrounded by assholes. Sometimes the ideas in a book can make a point or connection that you cannot. And assholes, unlike idiots, may be just as likely as you to read a book. If you're lucky, this might be the book that inspires them to be kinder, which will make the time you're forced to spend with them more bearable too.

Reason #3: You Can Help Me Make Money

Ok, I realize this is not particularly important to you, but my day job involves doing consulting and speaking ... and I love to help people and get paid for it. If you enjoyed this book, I guarantee you would enjoy working with me too. If that sounds like it might have value at your workplace, please get in touch with me directly and we can talk about how to make it happen – and how to make you a rock star for suggesting it in the first place.

ACKNOWLEDGEMENTS

For a book that unintentionally took four years to complete, it's not easy to know where to start when it comes to the people to thank behind it. Rather than follow tradition and save the best for last, I will instead *start* with the best and thank my amazing wife, Chhavi.

She has been a constant partner and inspiration ready to do everything from diving into line by line editing of this manuscript to helping co-found the publishing company behind it. I once joked in the opening dedication of my first book that she was my "accomplice" in raising our two boys. Ten years later I know she has that role in just about everything else too, and that is a beautiful thing.

On the editorial side, this book gave me the chance to come full circle by working with Terry Deal again, and her efforts to improve early drafts of this book helped make it so much better that it was when we started.

On our journey toward landing on the cover design, the quick work and artistic ethic of Christie Young made the process illuminating and fun. It's not every designer that will bake a clay sculpture in her oven just to visually illustrate a concept. Even though we didn't ultimately use that one, the journey to get there was more fun than I have had on any of my other books so far.

Anton Khodakovsky did wonderfully quick and professional work of turning this design into a beautiful interior layout and Lindsay and Sandy helped add all the polish and finishing details to make it as professional as it could be.

Shepherding this whole process and making sure the details were complete on time and to spec was my awesome Production Manager Marnie McMahon who expertly managed all the things that often fall through the cracks while making sure all our other projects were moving forward at the same speed.

I have to offer special thanks also to Rich Selby for being a force of detail in getting insane amounts of work done and jobs processed. Your willingness to be a partner and offer your expertise and dedication on this and so many other projects is more valuable than you sometimes realize.

When I say the advice in this book is the sort of thing you would not expect to hear from your parents, mine are no exception ... which makes me even more grateful to them for helping me learn these for myself.

In preparing for launch, I also enlisted the support of some very bright young people who agreed to join a launch team to help promote the book – and so a special thanks to all of them:

Akash Bhargava	Jared Hirsch	Kirin Singh
Neha Bhargava	Anjali Kalra	Viraj Suri
Varsha Bhargava	Surya Mehta	Anna Weidman
Jackie Chris	Ramses Rubio	Yiyi Zhang
Arjun Fischer	Nicholas Sabri	

I also need to share a special note of gratitude to Paresh Shah for not only reading the early manuscripts for the book, but offering exactly the sort of "this really sucks" brutally honest feedback from a place of kindness and helpfulness that every author needs to hear. Your insights helped shape the tone of the book and reminded me exactly who I was writing for, so thank you.

Finally, I would like to thank the many students and colleagues who have helped to shape the insights in this book without realizing it. Any insight is only as good as the experience which inspires it. I am lucky to get this sort of inspiration on a near daily basis … which ultimately made a book like this inevitable. In a good way.

INDEX

⌒⇭⌒

ENDNOTES

THIS IS NOT THE KIND OF BOOK TO HAVE EXHAUSTIVE ENDNOTES citing hundreds of primary and secondary sources. The primary source for most of the stories in this book is my life.

Still, I do mention a few research reports and articles throughout the book and for the more curious readers who want to read the full story (or the skeptical ones who want to sift through research for themselves), here is a short list of articles and research cited in this book.

1   To watch a video where I share this story in a live talk on stage, visit https://youtu.be/ThFJ76L7MB4

2   Malone-Kircher, Madison. "James Dyson on the 5,126 Vacuums That Didn't Work and the One That Finally Did." *The Vindicated*. N.p., 22 Nov. 2016. Web. 23 Feb. 2017.

3   "How To Be Resilient: 8 Steps To Success When Life Gets Hard." *Barking Up The Wrong Tree*. N.p., 14 Jan. 2015. Web. 23 Feb. 2017.

4   Bilton, Richard. "Apple 'Failing to Protect Chinese Factory Workers'." *BBC News*. BBC, 18 Dec. 2014. Web. 23 Feb. 2017.

5   Lebowitz, Shana. "From the Projects to a $2.3 Billion Fortune - the Inspiring Rags-to-Riches Story of Starbucks CEO Howard Schultz." *Business Insider*. Business Insider, 30 May 2015. Web. 23 Feb. 2017.

6   Baird, Frank. "Frank Baird, Walk Founder | Walk a Mile in Her Shoes®." *Frank Baird, Walk Founder | Walk a Mile in Her Shoes®*. Frank Baird, n.d. Web.23 Feb. 2017.

7   Johnson, Dirk. "A $42 Million Gift Aims at Improving Bedside Manner." *The New York Times*. The New York Times, 21 Sept. 2011. Web. 23 Feb. 2017.

8   Wharton School of the University of Pennsylvania. "Just-in-Time Education: Learning in the Global Information Age." *Wharton*. Wharton School of the University of Pennsylvania, 30 Aug. 2000. Web. 23 Feb. 2017.

9   Allison, Melissa. "Retiring CEO of Costco Takes a Look Back on His Legacy." *The Seattle Times*. The Seattle Times Company, 21 Dec. 2011. Web. 23 Feb. 2017.

10   "Cinnamon Bird." *Wikipedia*. Wikimedia Foundation, 26 Mar. 2016. Web. 23 Feb. 2017.

11   Jr., Keith Nelson. "Ellen Degeneres Beats out Fallon, Colbert as America's Favorite Talk Show Host." *Digital Trends*. N.p., 22 Jan. 2016. Web. 23 Feb. 2017.

12   Stevenson, Seth. "How to Succeed in Business: Hone Your Improv Comedy Skills." *Slate Magazine.* N.p., 30 Mar. 2014. Web. 23 Feb. 2017.

13   Psychol., Appl. Cognit. "Consequences of Erudite Vernacular Utilized Irrespective of Necessity: Problems with Using Long Words Needlessly." *(www.interscience. wiley.com) DOI: 10.1002/acp.1178 Consequences of Erudite Vernacular Utilized Irrespective of Necessity: Problems with Using Long Words Needlessly* (2005): 1-18. 31 Oct. 2005. Web. 23 Feb. 2017.

14   Strong, W. F. "The Airline That Started With A Cocktail Napkin." *Texas Standard.* N.p., 20 Apr. 2016. Web. 23 Feb. 2017.

15   Staff, NPR. "Don't Believe Facebook; You Only Have 150 Friends." *NPR.* NPR, 05 June 2011. Web. 23 Feb. 2017.

16   Hajo, Adam, and Adam D. Galinsky. "Enclothed Cognition." *Enclothed Cognition.* N.p., July 2008. Web. 23 Feb. 2017.

17   Bhargava, Rohit. "5 Rules of Social Media Optimization (SMO)." *Influential Marketing Blog.* N.p., 10 Aug. 2006. Web. 23 Feb. 2017.

18   Watch the full TEDTalk from Derek Sivers - https:// youtu.be/V74AxCqOTvg